PRINCIPLES
OF LOVE

HOW TO SUCCESSFULLY
PARENT YOUR ADULT
CHILDREN

PRINCIPLES
OF LOVE

HOW TO SUCCESSFULLY
PARENT YOUR ADULT
CHILDREN

GARTH A. HANSON, PH.D.
STEVE D. HANSON

Covenant Communications, Inc.

Cover image by Megumi Takamura © 2004 Photodisc Collection/GettyImages

Cover design copyrighted 2005 by Covenant Communications, Inc.

Published by Covenant Communications, Inc.
American Fork, Utah

Printed in Canada
First Printing: January 2005

11 10 09 08 07 06 05   10 9 8 7 6 5 4 3 2 1

ISBN 1-59156-705-X

To our children, who have taught us much

CONTENTS

INTRODUCTION

Our children are grown now, and we loved each phase of that growing-up process. Even so, as we look back, we remember that sometimes we caught ourselves almost wishing that we could skip ahead to the next stage of parenting because we wanted to avoid some of the frustrations and challenges that were inherent with the phase we were in. At those moments, we could only imagine a freer, less encumbered life when our children were older. Ironically, there are now times when we look back on those previous stages with yearning for their simplicity and lack of really serious problems.

Of course, each phase of parenting has its own unique challenges and rewards. And each phase is a learning experience because, by definition, we have not had that experience before. To forego any of these stages by wishing ourselves out of them would be to deny ourselves important knowledge that is probably necessary if we are to reach our divine potential.

Much of our learning simply comes through trial and error. Fortunately, *intent* or *desire* counts a lot when it comes to raising children. In this process of learning, very few "fatal" mistakes are made when we are *trying* to be good parents. Thank goodness! But that doesn't mean we shouldn't seek out assistance and counsel to supplement our learning experiences, especially when we are confronted with heart-wrenching challenges that sometimes, even often, crop up as we go about being parents.

That's really the purpose of this book—to give parents of adult children some reference points, based on the experiences of others, that will help them make better use of the knowledge they are gaining from their own unique challenges with their adult children. No one is an absolute expert on this subject, except our Heavenly Father. But we have had extensive experience both as parents of adult children and as counselors to many hundreds of young adults and parents of adult children. We have cried with and about our own children. We have cried with and about those we have counseled. We have felt the sorrow of parenting, and we have felt its joy. This book is a product of those experiences.

A few notes about terms used in this book. First, for simplicity, in some sections we use the words *adult children* to include older teens making mission, work, and education decisions, as well as younger teens in the chapter discussing pregnancy out of wedlock. Second, we use the word *parents* (plural) rather than *parent* (single). This is neither a slight against single parents nor indicative of an unawareness of their numbers or special challenges. It is simply a practical convenience. In fact, we have a particular empathy for single parents and are acutely aware of the additional burdens that are sometimes placed upon them. Interestingly, they enjoy some advantages as well, like not worrying about parental consensus. In any case, virtually all of the principles we describe and suggestions we make apply to single and married parents alike.

Throughout this book, we refer to a number of real-life situations. These examples are based on experiences that really did happen, though the names of the people have been changed. Most chapters contain a Question and Answer segment. Some of these questions come from individuals who have attended adult parenting seminars held by Dr. Garth Hanson over the years. Other questions have been created to help flesh out the principle being discussed. In these instances, the questions derive from actual counseling sessions we have either been a part of or have observed.

Section 1 of the book is titled "Ten Parenting Principles You Can't Ignore." It deals with principles that parents of adult children need to both understand and apply to effectively meet the unique challenges they face. Each chapter uses actual experiences to define a principle, provides a summarization of that principle and its ramifications, then concludes with a powerful series of questions and answers that are related to that principle. Section 1 closes with a succinct set of bylaws for parents with adult children.

Section 2 is titled "Let's Get Practical—Applying the Principles." It provides a step-by-step approach to implementing these ten principles in any parent–adult child relationship. The first chapter offers suggestions for defining and evaluating adult child challenges. The remaining chapters isolate specific, severe problems that many parents have with adult children. Practical counsel is given along with concrete examples, followed by questions and answers that let the reader see how the counsel can be realistically and effectively applied.

Whether we are parents or children, we are all sons and daughters of God who are learning through our experiences to be like Him. We hope that this book helps you as you seek to bless your adult children—and that you'll be blessed yourself in the process.

SECTION 1

TEN PARENTING PRINCIPLES YOU CAN'T IGNORE

"Programs blindly followed bring us to a discipline of doing good, but principles properly understood and practiced bring us to a disposition to do good."

(Glenn L. Pace, Ensign, May 1986, 24)

CHAPTER 1

FAMILIES ARE FOREVER—AND SO IS PARENTING

Principle 1: Parents never outlive their responsibility to their children.

"There is only one way to handle adult children. You teach them while they are growing up that they are no longer a part of your family after they turn eighteen. They are to pack their things and be ready to leave the house at that time. We are through with responsible relationships after that."

That statement kind of grates, doesn't it? We have heard such comments, though, and we have observed parents who feel that their parental charge ends when their children are "grown up." In shucking this God-given responsibility to raise their children by establishing some self-imposed time limit on it, parents push onto the shoulders of caring people, like priesthood and Relief Society leaders, their innate obligation as parents. Parental accountability lasts right up until the day we die, and beyond.

In 1995 the First Presidency and the Quorum of the Twelve issued a remarkable statement on the family. This unique document states in unequivocal terms the sacred and *eternal* nature of the family, and outlines the responsibilities that parents have for their children and for each other. Specifically it declares, "The divine plan of happiness enables family relationships to be perpetuated beyond the grave. Sacred ordinances and covenants . . . make it possible . . . for families to be united eternally. . . . Husband and wife have a solemn responsibility to love and care for each other and for their children" ("The Family: A Proclamation to the World," 1995).

Clearly, parents' worries and concerns for and interest in the well-being of their children should not end when the child turns a magic age or leaves home. Surely we know this intuitively. Eternal is eternal. We either have a *forever* family or we don't. If we do, that means that parents are forever too. Our responsibilities to our children, and our joys and sorrows in their actions, never cease. Our leaders have been forthright about this. One quote representative of many will be sufficient here. President Ezra Taft Benson said, "Fathers [and certainly mothers too], yours is an eternal calling from which you are never released. . . . [A] father's calling is eternal, and its importance transcends time. It is a calling for both time and eternity" ("To the Fathers in Israel," *Ensign,* November 1987, 48).

Our accountability before God and our proximity to His divine status as a *Heavenly* Father or an *Eternal* Father must be significantly affected by the degree of our willingness to assume our never-ending parenting responsibilities. Indeed, the earthly parental process seems to be the type and shadow of—and the way to becoming—heavenly fathers and heavenly mothers. Exaltation is the result of successfully following that path.

CHANGING RESPONSIBILITIES

While parental responsibility never ceases, parental responsibilities do change. At the birth of a child, parents provide for her every need. As the child grows, the amount of parental involvement necessary for the child to sustain life decreases. Over time, what that involvement *should be* becomes harder for parents to determine. That challenge is made even more complicated as the child has an increasingly significant input as to just what she wants (or will allow) her parents' involvement to be. By the time a child has reached adulthood, the escalating complexity of the timing, extent, and direction of parental involvement in the child's life sometimes causes parents to give up. It's just too much. As a result, they either assume a very passive role in their relationships with the adult child or stop those relationships altogether. When this happens, everybody loses.

Most parents are capable of making the appropriate adjustments as their children move from childhood to adulthood. What is required is the *desire* to do so. A lack of parental willingness to continue on with what they have started is usually a manifestation of extreme selfishness.

EXTENDED FAMILY RESPONSIBILITY

Parents will spend many more years with their offspring as adults than they will with them when they are young. Not only will they be involved with their adult children, but also in the lives of all of those who come into the family as their children form their own families. This expanded circle includes their spouses, children, and perhaps even stepchildren. Each of these relationships creates additional challenges for parents of adult children. These added people are part of the eternal family too, and parental responsibility extends to them as well.

A number of years ago, Raymond Hanson (Garth's father and Steve's grandfather) stood in front of his family who were gathered at a reunion. He was in his nineties at the time and had outlived three wives. His descendants numbered over two hundred, most of whom were there. While physically feeble, Raymond spoke clearly and with power. He expressed his love for all of his family, including the "in-laws" and the "steps." He bore a strong testimony of the gospel and invited those who were having spiritual challenges to change their lives so that the families could be together eternally. It was an emotionally charged moment for all who were there as we watched the patriarch of our family magnify his role as a parent right up to the end of his life.

We believe that that is the way it ought to be.

PONDERING THE PRINCIPLE

Recognizing the eternal nature of parenthood is an important first step in creating the kind of ongoing relationships that will allow parents to bless the lives of their adult children. Establishing eternal relationships takes significant time and concerted effort, as well as a willingness to do it.

- Parents have a sacred responsibility to "love and care" for their adult children.
- Rejecting one's parental role with an adult child unfairly pushes that responsibility onto someone else.
- Parent abrogation of responsibility for an adult child is usually a selfish decision.
- Successful family relationships have much to do with our happiness in this life and in the life to come.
- Parenting is an eternal responsibility.
- Exaltation means becoming a *heavenly parent.*
- Parenting responsibilities never cease, but they change with the age of the child.
- Parental involvements with adult children are often complex and their extent and direction hard to determine.
- Parental responsibilities extend to the spouses of adult children, to grandchildren, and to stepgrandchildren.

Our proximity to our Heavenly Father seems to be measured by how closely we follow His example as mothers and fathers to our own children. This implies that we not only strive to be good parents, but that we willingly seek to magnify our parental role throughout our lives.

QUESTIONS & ANSWERS

Q What is wrong with turning children out of the home at age eighteen or twenty-one or whenever and letting them fend for themselves?

A Nothing. In fact, that might be the right thing to do. What is wrong is when parents cast their children from their home and then forget about them. Contact should be maintained wherever possible, and a lifelong *active* relationship needs to be fostered.

Q What can I do to help my children after they leave home? Don't they have their agency?

A Yes, they do. But they need encouragement, support (sometimes physical and monetary, as well as spiritual and emotional), and a friend they know they can depend on. That's what parents are for. You can help them make good decisions too. Adult children like to know your opinions, and they follow your counsel much more than you might think.

Q My daughter and I have never been good friends. She is now married and has children, and we still aren't good friends. We have worked from separate pages almost from the beginning. I think we both love each other, but we do not get along well. What should I do?

A The key here is to maintain a relationship. A fragile relationship is better than none at all. It usually takes more energy to deal with a fragile relationship than with a good one, and it isn't as much fun. Life is certainly better if we can be friends with our children, but it doesn't always happen. What you can do is *respect* one another. Work on that. Spend time with each other, being careful about what you say. Some rewards will come.

Q It seems as though your kind of parenting is making work for yourselves in places perhaps you ought not to be. Isn't it better to let your adult children make lives for themselves without butting in?

A You are right; it is work. But active parenting is not synonymous with interfering or butting into the lives of adult children. Active parenting means you stay in touch. You visit them as often as is reasonable. You provide a support mechanism for them. You do not have to be intrusive to be involved, and wise parents will tailor the degree of their involvement to the desires and needs of their children.

Q What is the worst relationship you have ever seen between parents and their adult children?

A Where the adult children don't want any contact with their parents and refuse to allow them into their home, or where the parents refuse any contact with their adult children. We have devoted a chapter in section 2 of this book to this kind of problem. It can be dealt with, and sometimes relationships can be reestablished.

Q When we go to visit our children, we stay at a local hotel rather than in their home. We don't want to be a burden to them, and we also like our private time. Our children keep asking us to stay with them. What do you suggest?

A Stay with them. You are missing the most important part of the visit—the early morning and the late evening. That time with the grandchildren is priceless, and that is usually the time when meaningful conversations between you and your children will occur. You are also sending an unintended signal to your children—that you are more comfortable outside their home. That signal can keep your relationship with your children from being all that you would like it to be. How would you feel if your children stayed at a hotel when they visited you? (Maybe you'd better not answer that.)

Q We really are very busy in our life, and we don't have the time to do all we should. What can we do to be better at parenting?

A Well, the first thing you need to do is make it a priority. The challenge in this life seems to be more one of choosing between good and better than between good and bad things. That means we have to prioritize. When you decide that being a good parent to your adult child is one of the most important things you can do, you will find you will *make* time to do the things you *need* to do in that relationship. That does not necessarily mean that you will have time to do all of the things you *want* to do, though.

Q What can we do to have our adult children keep in better contact with us? We call them from time to time and try to visit them once a year or more (they live out of state), but they never call us and never come to visit.

A Why don't you try getting a personal toll-free 800 number. It isn't that expensive, and it won't cost your children anything to call you. They are probably like you were when you had small children—watching every penny. With little children around, their lives are pretty hectic, and they just may forget to call. You might want to plan on talking with them regularly (like once a week), and if they don't call you, call them. At this stage of their lives it is a lot easier for you to visit them than for them to visit you. Just do what you need to do to keep sufficient contact. It's worth the price.

Q One of our sons-in-law calls us by our first names. We both feel awkward about that and wish he would call us Mom and Dad. I know we aren't his real parents, but he is part of our family, and we want to have a parental relationship with him. What would you advise?

A Tell him that he can call you anything he wants to, but you would prefer that he call you Mom and Dad. If he continues to call you by your first names, let it drop. There is a natural reluctance to call anyone but your own parents by those names. Usually, however, children will begin using mother/father names with their in-law parents after they become close to them, especially if they know how they feel. But that takes time. You can be sure, though, that until he feels comfortable enough to use those names, your relationship with him will probably not be as close as you would like it to be.

Q How do you get close to your grandchildren? Ours are nice enough, but when we visit they say, "Hi!" and run off. They don't seem to like to be around us all that much.

A How much attention do you pay to them? Sometimes our calls and visits are too focused on the adults, and the children get left out. It doesn't take long before they either don't feel wanted in the conversation or are not interested in it. Try paying "adultlike" attention to your grandchildren when you visit and when you call. Ask them what they are doing and listen. Ask open-ended questions so they have a chance to express themselves. Write them letters and send them birthday cards and Christmas presents. That helps. When you visit with them, try to spend some individual time with each one. That could be a game, a story, or a drive down to McDonald's for a treat. If they know you are interested in them, they will be interested in you.

Q My husband says that I give too many gifts to my grandchildren. He could be right, but how do we know?

A   When your grandchildren head to your suitcase to see what you brought them before giving you a hug and a kiss, you know you've gone too far. If the primary reason they are glad to see you is because of your gifts, it's time to change. If this is the case, you should consider buying gifts for them in consultation with their parents so you are getting them what they need rather than what will get the biggest instant positive reaction.

Q   Do you think we can be as effective in dealing with our adult children as we were when they were little? They had to listen to us then.

A   You can be just as effective and even more so. They *had* to listen to you then. Hopefully, now that they are older and have some experience, they will *want* to listen to you.

Q   When our children first got married, my wife and I only gave presents to our children for their birthdays, rather than to their spouses. We figured that the spouses' families would take care of their own children. Some of our children didn't like that, so we have started giving presents to our in-law children too, but they are more token gifts than substantial ones. Some of our children are still unhappy about that. What do you think we should do?

A   Your children's spouses are part of your family now and should be treated as such. Doing what you are doing (or what you did) tells them that you do not consider them "family." If you want to have good relationships with them, with your own children, and ultimately with your grandchildren, you'd better start accepting your in-laws for who they are—members of *your* family—and then show it.

CHAPTER 2

AGENCY: THEIRS AND YOURS

Principle 2: Parents and children have the ability and the right to make choices independent of the other's decisions and actions.

You can't spend more than five minutes driving on any road in the country without seeing a bumper sticker on some car that says, "My Child Was Student of the Month at (*Fill-In-the-Blank*) School!" Of course, the purpose of the bumper sticker isn't just to make the child feel good. He or she isn't riding around in the car all day looking out the window and smiling knowingly at passersby. But sometimes Mom or Dad is. You know what he or she is probably thinking too: *My child's smart—it's in the genes. I've taught her everything she knows. She's my clone. I've done a bang-up job of being a parent, and here's the proof. Ahh, by the way, where's* your *bumper sticker?*

Just once we'd like to see a bumper sticker that says, "My Child Failed Algebra!" or, "My Son Is in Juvenile Hall!" But that's not likely. Parents are naturally more *outwardly* inclined to take responsibility for the "good" things their children do than they are for those things that aren't so good. But if we accept that parents are completely responsible for children turning out "good," then we also have to accept that parents are completely responsible for children that turn out not-so-good. Are parents responsible for the actions (good or bad) of their children? Consider the following story.

Several years ago, Bob was talking to his stake president. The stake president had just ended an interview with Bob's twenty-one-year-old son, who had recently returned from a mission in a third-world country. The stake president was effusive in his compliments about the son and concluded by saying to Bob, "You must be a marvelous father to have raised a son like that."

Bob's first impulse was to accept the compliment as being deserved (another bumper sticker for his car). After all, he and his wife, Janice, spent lots of time with their children as they were growing up, held family home evenings regularly, taught the scriptures in their home, attended the temple often, accepted and tried to magnify Church callings, and encouraged their son to go on a mission from the time he was little. They listened well, talked out problems, disciplined reasonably and consistently, and tried to live exemplary lives themselves.

But then the face of his daughter Enid flashed into his mind. She was ending her second marriage; had challenges with dishonesty, promiscuity, and drugs; and had never been able to hold a job for longer than a few weeks. She had been raised in the same home and had been treated, as far as Bob knew, the same as his son.

Bob didn't take the bumper sticker. Instead his response surprised his stake president and himself: "If you give me credit for what my son's doing, you have to give me the blame for what my daughter's done. I don't think I deserve either one."

To what extent, if any, are parents responsible for their children's deeds? That's not an easy question to answer. In fact, it's an ongoing question that "experts" debate all the time. Why are we the way we are? To what extent do our genes influence our behavior? How much does the environment within which we were raised affect our ultimate mental and emotional makeup?

Further, as Latter-day Saints, our gospel perspective requires that we add two additional critical considerations as we seek to determine ultimate responsibility for actions and choices: the eternal nature of man, and our God-given moral agency. To understand that we did not *begin* with our earthly birth and that we have an innate moral agency is to know that our personalities and dispositions may be *affected* by our family environment (as well as a million other things), but not ultimately *determined* by it (or them). We came to earth with our own individual characteristics and talents. Any parent who has more than one child knows this to be the case without having to be taught it. They can see that each child is different—really different.

So why do our adult children do what they do? Perhaps the answer involves all of the above reasons—genetics, environment, man's eternal nature, and agency. Certainly any one of these variables can temporarily affect our children. But if the doctrines of agency, man's eternal nature, and judgment are true, then we must ultimately be responsible for our choices. And whatever the degree of influence parents' actions (or any other influence, for that matter) have had on the way their adult children behave, their children still have the ability to choose *now* how they will act.

That is not to say that parents do not play a significant role in helping their children develop attributes and habits that will bless (or hinder) their lives. They do. But it is also true that in those things which are eternally significant, sons and daughters of God must be held accountable for their own choices. Otherwise there is no moral agency (see, for example, 2 Ne. 2:10–16, 21, 26–29).

What we do or do not do as parents does not, cannot determine our children's salvation. Our role as parents is limited to (1) teaching our children by precept and example the reality of the joy and peace that comes in following Christ, and (2) assisting them when we feel it is in their and our best interest to do so. In essence, we only have the power to be heavenly parents. We cannot make our children become heavenly children. Recognizing their agency and our limitations to persuade increases our potential effectiveness in teaching them "correct principles" and also reduces much of the unnecessary stress that comes when we wrongly assume responsibility for their errant behavior. The following story illustrates this principle.

Linda sat in a counseling session with two psychologists and her rebellious daughter, Carrie. Linda was nearly beside herself with her inability to control her teenager's deviant and defiant behavior. In her mind, she was somehow to blame for Carrie's mixed-up views of life and for the unbearable antipathy that her daughter seemed to feel toward her. Linda was willing to do anything that would improve the situation; she just needed to know what it was she was doing to cause Carrie's horrible attitude.

After some time had passed, one of the psychologists looked at Carrie and asked, "Is there anything at all your mother can do to get you to like her?" Without hesitation, Carrie replied emphatically, "No. Not a thing."

The psychologist then turned to Linda and asked, "Does that answer your question as to who is at fault here?"

The realization for Linda that she was not responsible for Carrie's choices was life-changing. While knowing this didn't stop Linda's tears over Carrie's self-destructive behavior, it did substantially reduce the sense of futility that had been her constant companion through the months of trying to change her own behavior in order to "make" Carrie "better." Linda's periods of debilitating depression decreased, and her own peace gradually returned, even though Carrie's behavior did not change significantly.

Linda began to work more on trying to increase her own proximity to the Savior and less on trying to please her struggling daughter. This focus brought her both a sense of accomplishment and control. Carrie's actions became less and less a factor in determining Linda's happiness, and that, paradoxically, gradually improved the relationship between mother and daughter. Linda was learning to become a better parent by controlling the only things she could control—her own actions, feelings, and thoughts.

PONDERING THE PRINCIPLE

Recognition of the right and ability of parents and children to make choices independent of each other's decisions and actions is critical in establishing and maintaining any viable parent–adult child relationship.

- Children's actions do not necessarily make a statement about how they were raised.
- Parents' actions may affect their posterity for good or for ill.
- Parents can influence, but cannot ultimately control, what their children do.
- Parents' actions will not determine their children's eternal salvation.
- Children's actions will not determine their parents' eternal salvation.
- Neither children nor parents can take the right to choose away from the other.

Understanding the reality of moral agency and its ramifications helps parents to know what they can and cannot do in their relationships with their adult children. This leads them to know what they should or should not be doing in those relationships. There is no principle that is more fundamental.

QUESTIONS & ANSWERS

Q Why do I have to be the parent of a disobedient and inconsiderate adult child? Why does this happen to me?

A Why not you? All children, no matter to whom they are born, have agency. They can choose how they behave. That's just the way it is.

Q What can I do to help after my child leaves home? Isn't each child responsible for his or her choices?

A Yes, they are responsible, but the role of parents is to encourage, support, communicate, and befriend adult children as they progress. We believe our role as parents is to assist our adult children in making good decisions. That role is more intense with our children in the earlier years of their adulthood than it is later, but it never ceases.

Q We have worked to teach responsibility to all of our children. Five of them have learned it well and are doing very nicely. We don't know what happened to the other one, but he is really not doing well. Where did we go wrong?

A We can't answer that completely, but your son's agency plays an important part here. Many children believe that they can do what they please regardless of what anyone else tells them to do, especially parents—or so it seems. We can't tell you that you did nothing wrong, but we can say that your son has his agency to do wrong. Do yourself a favor and get some peace into your life. Keep doing all you can do, but realize that his actions now are not your fault. Keep him in your prayers, keep in touch with him, and get on with life. That's tough to do, but it's the best thing—for you and for him.

Q How do you deal with adult children who blame you for everything that is wrong in their lives?

A The prescription is easy, but swallowing the medicine is a challenge. We have a very hard time with adult children who verbally abuse their parents for any reason, and this is what you are experiencing. These young adults are very often in trouble, which makes the problem worse. Nevertheless, they should respect you. You should sit down with this adult child and let him or her know that this verbal abuse has to stop or some privileges will be withdrawn, like living in your house or receiving financial support. If the child is not living with you and will not stop the verbal abuse, you should consider reducing your contact with him or her for a while. But always love them.

Q Is it true that you cannot do much to help your children create personal habits when they grow older?

A Probably not. You can still encourage these positive habits when your family gets together. There is no question that you would likely have had more success if you had provided that training when your children were in your home, but that time has passed. You need to deal with the situation now. Don't preach too much. Just set the example yourself. It is possible to make a difference no matter what the age. Your example might have a positive effect.

Q My son has done about everything wrong that is possible. He doesn't seem to care about anything but himself. I am praying that he will change. Is this wrong to ask Heavenly Father to change my son's heart? Is that praying to take away his agency?

A It is not wrong to plead for our children's eternal welfare. We, of course, cannot ask Heavenly Father to take away someone's agency, but we can pray that a loved one will be brought to see that what he or she is doing is destructive. We can ask God to bless our children with understanding and a testimony of truth. We can pray for help that we will know what to do to help them. We can pray that the Lord will bless our children with experiences that will allow them to know who they are. We do not have the right to dictate in our prayers how a child will respond to such an experience, but we do have the right to ask that our child have potentially life-changing experiences. Be patient and keep praying for your son.

Q Since our daughter has married we feel like we've lost any control we had over how she behaves. She and her husband are both completely irresponsible. They don't keep appointments, they don't keep promises, and they don't pay their debts. What should we do?

A There is probably not a lot you can do at this point in time. They have a right to make their choices, and you do not have a right to prevent them from doing so. What you can do is to choose not to enable their bad habits by lending them money or excusing their actions. You may want to ask them if they would be receptive to some counsel if you have not already done so. If they don't want it, don't give it. It will probably be counterproductive for you to harp on this. The chances are that sooner or later they will learn that their present behavior will not make them very happy. Pray that they will learn that sooner.

Q I am a single mother who was widowed when my children were teenagers. They are grown now and married. I have met a man whom I want to marry, but my children are against it. They bring up all kinds of reasons why I shouldn't marry him, all of which I think are baseless. I think they just don't want anyone to replace their father. I don't want to alienate my children, but I love this man and I want to marry him. What should I do?

A You should look at your children's comments as counsel only. They cannot dictate to you any more than you can dictate to them. You should make your decision based on what will be best for you. Your relationship with your children will suffer only if they choose to let it, and that is out of your control.

Q My stepson is twenty-two and served an honorable mission. I bought a car for him to use, and he lives at home with his mother and me. He has been going to school and he works, but he has been going with a nonmember girl and stays out every night until ridiculous hours in the morning (like 3:00 to 4:00 A.M.). Two nights now he hasn't come home. He said he fell asleep watching movies. He claims that he is not doing anything wrong, but he won't listen to our counsel because he says he is an adult. My relationship with him has been fragile anyway ever since his mother and I were married two years before he went on his mission. I don't want to strain our relationship any further, but I don't think it's right for us to sit back and do nothing. My wife and I are stumped. Any advice?

A   Your stepson needs to act like an adult if he wants to be treated like an adult. You don't own him, but you do own the car. You probably can't realistically put a curfew on him, but you can put a curfew on the car. Make it really reasonable to begin with, like 1:00 or 2:00 A.M. If the car is not home by then, ground the car for twenty-four hours. If there is a continual violation of curfew, increase the amount of time the car is grounded. You and your wife should present this curfew to your son jointly so he knows it is coming from both of you. It takes two to establish a good relationship. When you are doing what you can do to help your stepson (and making it more difficult for him to carry out self-destructive behavior is helping him), you are doing all you can do. Hopefully, he will eventually respond in a positive way, but that is his choice.

Q   I am a single mom and have been for ten years. I have two sons, eighteen and twenty. I have told them over the years that they are the men in the home since my husband is gone. We have worked together to make our family work, and we have done quite well, but things are changing. They are going their separate ways, but they are still acting like they are in charge of me and my assets. What should I do to get control back?

A   You are seeing on a firsthand basis why a single parent must not relinquish control of his or her life to the children. It is one thing to solicit their extra cooperation when a spouse is lost either through death or divorce; it is quite another to put them in the place of that absent spouse. What you need to do is sit down with your sons and tell them you appreciate all that they have done to help you over the past years but it is time for you to take charge of yourself and your resources. Tell them that you would like to ask for their counsel from time to time and would even listen to their unsolicited advice, but their input from now on will be just counsel, and you will be making the ultimate decisions. Ask them to honor your request and your right to direct your own life.

Q My daughter came home from college graduated and single. She loves living in our nice home, and we love having her here. However, she refuses to tell me where she is going or when or if she will be home that night. She insists that she is old enough to make her own decisions. What can I do? I don't know when to fix meals, when to expect her, or anything. This is destroying our relationship.

A Your daughter is old enough to make her own decisions, and she is also old enough to be considerate. Your requests are reasonable and have to do with the management of your home, not the agency of your daughter. Explain to her that you would expect anyone who lives in your home to be communicative with you regarding these things so you can plan accordingly and won't have to worry. Go over each area you feel she should give you information about and explain why it is important for you to know it. It is your home, and you have the right to set your expectations. She needs to know that she has the responsibility to abide by those expectations if she wants to live there. Getting this out on the table now is the way to preserve your relationship.

Q Where does my children's agency end and mine begin?

A Good question. The answer is simple in concept, but not always easy to apply. Whenever your child seeks to make a choice that involves (or depends upon) your having to make a choice, her agency has just ended and yours has begun. She can go no further without your making a choice, nor can she take away from you the right to make that choice in the way that you desire. For example, if your married son and his wife make a decision to purchase a home but expect a loan from you to subsidize their down payment, it will be your choice, not theirs, that will determine whether they can proceed.

CHAPTER 3

CASTING YOUR CHILDREN OUT OF THE GARDEN OF EDEN

Principle 3: Positive change generally does not occur until parents allow their children to experience the consequences of bad decisions.

Lance Smith, a young adult living at home, was doing just about everything wrong he could do. He lied, stole, cheated, and used drugs and alcohol. He was immoral and seemed completely indifferent to how his actions were affecting his parents. His mother and father had tried everything that they knew to help him. For several years they had been patient and forgiving. They persuaded him to see a professional counselor, but after a session or two, he refused to go. He never did agree to see his bishop. No matter what they tried, it didn't work. Finally, the inevitable happened. Lance was arrested.

The phone rang at Lance's home and his mother answered. "Hi, Mom, this is Lance. I am in jail, and they won't let me out until you or Dad come and get me. Please hurry!"

Mom was shocked, even panicked, but didn't say anything. Lance pleaded again, "Mom, please hurry! This is not a nice place to be!"

Mom didn't say anything for a long time, and then she quietly asked, "Lance, are you guilty of the charges?"

"Well, Mom, I really wasn't as involved as the police say that I was."

"Lance, are you guilty?"

"Well, Mom, I guess I am."

Then with all of the courage she could muster, Mom replied, "Well, Lance, I'm sorry that you are. I guess that you will have to work through this by yourself. Call me when you get it all worked out." Mom hung up the phone and fell apart.

Two very long days passed. Finally, Lance called, and Mom and Dad went to the police station to pick him up. A few more days passed and the phone rang again. This time it was an attorney. "Hello, Mrs. Smith. I am Mark Johnson. I helped Lance with his legal problems while he was in custody. I just wanted to speak with you to see how you wanted to work out my compensation for helping Lance get out of jail."

At first Lance's mother was troubled. Finances were tight, and she was surprised by the call. She paused a minute, then said, "Mr. Johnson, I appreciate what you did to help Lance, but you are talking to the wrong person. I did not hire you. You did not help me; you helped Lance. If you want compensation for your efforts, I think you ought to talk to Lance." She hung up the phone.

Sometime later, Lance came to his parents asking for a "donation" to pay his legal bill, but the donation did not come. Lance had to go back to the attorney and work out a payback plan, which he followed. After many months of payments, Lance paid Mr. Johnson off. He finally served an honorable mission and is doing very well as a student in a major university. He is paying for much of his education himself, and his relationship with his parents couldn't be better. He will tell you today that the actions of his very brave and very frightened mother turned his life around.

Unfortunately, not all stories have such an immediately happy ending. However, many (maybe most) stories do, if you wait long enough and if you are trying to do the right thing.

Parents are required to teach their children responsibility for their actions. This is almost always a very hard thing to do and often may involve what seems to be a temporary abandonment. In a very real sense, parents can interfere with their adult children's progress if they cloud their children's ability to see and experience consequences by trying to protect them from those consequences. Our prototype here is Heavenly Father and His response to Adam and Eve's partaking of the forbidden fruit. They did it, and He cast them out of the Garden of Eden.

This consequence not only carried with it an unforgettable message to obey God, but contained a latent teaching experience that could be used by Adam and Eve, if they chose, to become more like God. This would result in Adam and Eve's ultimate reunification with Heavenly

Father and in obtaining knowledge they did not possess before the transgression, knowledge that was necessary if they were ever to become like their own divine parents. In allowing the consequence of His children's actions to follow them, Heavenly Father was blessing more than punishing. And so it should be with us.

If God had not allowed Adam and Eve to experience the consequence of their action, they would have remained in the Garden of Eden, and "never should have had seed, and never should have known good and evil, and the joy of [their] redemption, and the eternal life which God giveth unto all the obedient" (Moses 5:11). In essence, they would have lived forever *in their sins,* effectively held back from ever reaching their divine potential.

If Lance's mother had not followed this important principle, it is doubtful that Lance would have turned his life around. And as well-meaning as his parents may have been by protecting him from a very challenging situation, they would, in fact, have slowed his progression. They would have loved him to his spiritual death. A real paradox, huh?

GRACE AND CONSEQUENCES

But what about parental grace? Mirroring our Heavenly Father would be to extend grace to our children as He does to us. After all, He did provide us with a Savior. Is there a contradiction here? The whole intent of the Atonement (grace) seems to be to keep us from suffering the natural consequences of our actions (see D&C 19:16). Shouldn't parents be willing to offer that same grace to their children?

The seeming contradiction between receiving grace and experiencing consequences is resolved when we consider the restrictions or qualifications that God places on His grace. God's grace comes only after:

- We have done all that we can do for ourselves (see 2 Ne. 25:23).
- We have recognized what we have done to bring on the consequences and we *want* to change (see Moro. 10:32; D&C 19:16).

- We are humble because of our weaknesses (see Ether 12:27).
- The promise is that His grace will be *sufficient* for us (see Ether 12:27; Moro. 10:32).

This seems to indicate that grace will never replace a consequence or experience that is necessary to teach us something we *need to know*. Grace will be bestowed only after we have done all that we can do to improve our spiritual, physical, mental, or emotional well-being.

Once again, Heavenly Father becomes our model as we apply His parameters in meting out grace to our adult children. But unlike Him, we don't have a perfect knowledge of all things. For us, it is tough to know *when* to apply grace, *how much* grace to give, and *what* that grace should be. Asking these questions may help:

- Are our children doing everything they can do to solve their own problems?
- Are they making "acceptable" progress in the right direction?
- Is their attitude what it should be?
- Will our efforts really help?
- What do we feel spiritually prompted to do?

Perhaps a key here is for parents to strive to always desire what will be best for their children, and then be willing to do what is necessary, no matter what sacrifice may be required or how difficult it may be for them personally. Remember, the Savior both gave and withheld. Always, always, He was willing to personally sacrifice for another, *if* that would help.

PONDERING THE PRINCIPLE

We have experiences so we can learn. That is a major purpose for this mortal probation. Part of this learning process involves seeing on a firsthand basis the consequences of actions. If we do not experience the consequences, we cannot learn what we have been sent here to learn. Our eternal progress can be affected detrimentally as a result.

- Parents must be willing to say no when it will be in the best interests of their adult child.
- Preventing our children from experiencing the consequences of their actions is usually counterproductive and often spiritually destructive to the child.
- Parental assistance should be measured and prayerfully considered as to its potential ramifications.
- Parents should always have the welfare of their adult children in mind and be willing to sacrifice to the extent that it will help.

Parents have the responsibility both to allow adult children to learn from the consequences of their actions, and to provide appropriate assistance that will help them make positive progress as a result of their challenges.

QUESTIONS & ANSWERS

Q How do I keep my son from getting angry with me when I say no to him?

A You don't. But don't let him lay the guilt trip on you. Meet with him and let him know how you feel. Don't get drawn into a confrontation. Stay calm and ignore the tantrum. The problem is mostly his, not yours. Keep the love flowing his way.

Q My son is eighteen and a senior in high school. Because he is legally an adult, he signed to have his grades given only to him and not sent home to us. He is refusing to let us see his grades. What can I do?

A Tell him if he wants to be independent, he can start paying for rent, board, mileage on the car he's using, gasoline, and car insurance. We bet you get to see his grades from now on.

Q Our daughter lives with us and is a good kid, but she is totally irresponsible. She won't keep her room clean, help around the house, or do what she says she will do. We've tried everything (I think) and nothing seems to work for long. She doesn't do anything that would warrant kicking her out of our house. She is going to school and is active in church. What do you think we should do?

A Responsibility can be taught, but sometimes it takes a while. How much effort you put into it depends on how serious you think the problem is and what the long-term ramifications are. Irresponsibility in small things can eventually develop into "biggies" in the future, or it can mean nothing but a need to learn how to prioritize or organize. One thing you might try is to meet with her, go over your concerns, and get her to agree to certain responsibilities (e.g., cleaning her room, doing assigned jobs around the house, etc.). Then go over what you are giving her now, like free room and board, use of an automobile, tuition, or whatever. Explain that these are things you want to do for her, but you expect her cooperation in return. If she doesn't do what she agrees to do (and what you expect her to do), tell her that some of these benefits are going to be withheld. For example, for each job she misses, you might subtract twenty dollars off the amount of tuition you will pay; or, for each day she misses cleaning her room, she will miss a day using the car. Write this all out so there are no questions as to what is expected and what the consequences are. Try to make the consequences fit the action.

Q Are you saying that you should not give everything you have to save your own flesh and blood from some destroying force?

A That is not what we are saying. You should be willing to give everything you have if it will *save* them. But you want your sacrifice to actually help them. Sometimes the very best thing you can do for your children is to tell them no; and sometimes the very worst thing you can do is to tell them yes.

Q When my wife and I go to our daughter's house, my wife just takes over and cooks the meals, washes the clothes, tends the grandchildren, and so on. I think my son-in-law resents our coming. I have talked to my wife about this, but she thinks I am silly. What do you think?

A You are not being silly. Some parents underestimate their adult children's abilities, so they take charge. Others just want to help and try to lighten the load. Either way, such actions can cause resentment or even an unhealthy feeling of dependency on the part of your children. You might want to talk to your wife about remembering that you are guests in their home and need to act accordingly. Help, but don't take over.

Q How do I know when I have tried enough with my errant adult child who has put our family through near-bankruptcy, ruin, and unmentionable embarrassment, not to mention what he has done to himself? I really don't think he will ever change.

A Maybe it's time to reduce your level of trying if you have been putting all of your energies and resources into solving this child's problems. That doesn't mean you stop trying altogether. There are some things you can do, like keeping him in your prayers and communicating with him if he will let you. It sounds like you have done what you can; now it's time to get on with your life.

CHAPTER 4

TAKE A LOOK AT WHERE YOU'RE COMING FROM

Principle 4: The Savior's way is the only one that ultimately works.
His motivation is love; His technique is invitation.

A number of years ago, a great-grandmother who was in her nineties and her widowed daughter, Emily, were playing dominoes with their grandson. Mother and daughter were entertaining him with stories about their lives in New York City just after the turn of the century. After a number of family stories, Emily related the account of her first date with her husband-to-be. He had taken her to Coney Island, a beachfront amusement park. Emily described in detail the rides that they went on and the fun that they had. She said they went on the parachute drop ride, and as they were being lifted high above the park, her fiancé would lean over the side of the gondola and spit on the crowd below.

The grandson laughed. The great-grandmother didn't. She immediately looked up from the game with anger flaming from her eyes. In a quivering voice that did not diminish the force of her words, she said to her seventy-plus-year-old daughter, "Emily, if I had known that, you never would have married that man!"

Like Emily's mother, some parents have a tendency to direct their children's lives no matter how old their adult children are. And, frankly, their motivation is suspect, for when it comes to dealing with adult children, parents' motivations and methods are closely tied together.

For example, an inclination to use force and intimidation in a parent-child relationship is usually more a manifestation of parental pride than genuine concern for the child. By constraining the child into "acceptable" paths, parents seek to avoid potential pride-piercing embarrassment (uncontrolled children do that to you, you know), while at the same time they enhance their own image. Their honor and glory is in not "losing" any of their children because they have not "allowed" that to happen. (Somebody tried this before, by the way, and he failed miserably [see Moses 4:1, 3]). The result of such motives and methods is more often than not a fragile relationship peppered with parental Pyrrhic victories, and the ultimate outcome is neither heavenly parents nor heavenly children.

When _love is the overriding parental motivation_, methods used to direct adult children tend to be "softer." Compulsion is replaced by invitation, intimidation by persuasion. And while the immediate outcome of such actions is less predictable, the long-term effects are almost always more positive. Why? Because it is the _right_ way. It is Christ's way.

·THE GIFT OF CHARITY

Parental intent and desire are everything. When that desire is charity-inspired, the likelihood of parents' actions and words actually blessing their children increases, in spite of a parental lack of wisdom, knowledge, and "good" parenting techniques. Adult children can _feel_ that intent, and it registers with them.

In the Book of Mormon, charity is defined as the "pure love of Christ" (Moro. 7:47). It apparently is not innate within us, but must be energetically sought after through fervent prayer and by following Jesus Christ completely. In essence, we must want it and do what is necessary to receive it. It is then given to us by God (see Moro. 7:47–48). Usually, we receive this gift in the same degree that our own lives are conforming to Christ's. It is a line-upon-line, precept-upon-precept kind of thing.

What is the pure love of Christ? It seems to be a completely self-less motivation to help others (see Moses 1:39). It is possessing the attributes of long-suffering, kindness, humility, righteousness, patience, truth-seeking, benevolence, and hope, among others (see 1 Cor. 13:4–7). These traits are found in parents who are striving to love their adult children with the "pure love of Christ." And parents develop that love as they attempt to manifest these attributes in their relationships with their children.

It takes great effort to develop this love, but parents who are striving for it will be more consistent in doing what is best for their adult children. And when their actions are charity based, the bond between parents and children will usually increase, regardless of how negatively children view those actions. In most cases, that tether of love will hold until children have experiences that will either confirm to them the rightness of their parents' actions or bring them to forgive their parents' miscues.

PONDERING THE PRINCIPLE

Parental methods are usually a manifestation of parent motives. Pride-centered motives give birth to authoritarian techniques, including browbeating, coercion, and force. Charity-motivated parents, on the other hand, will seek to *persuade* their adult children to take responsible paths and *invite* them to live productive, righteous lives.

- Parents do not own their children.
- Parents who use dictatorial methods often alienate their adult children and create deep-seated feelings of bitterness, resentment, and hatred.
- Parental force does not work in the long run.
- Charity-based parental actions, even if awkward and off the mark, will usually bless the children.
- Parent selflessness is a key to establishing desirable parent–adult child relationships.
- Charity is a gift and must be sought after.
- Love-motivated parents establish ties with their adult children that are not easily broken.
- Charity-inspired methods are the only ones that ultimately work.

All parents wrestle with their motivations. Developing Christ's pure love is a process, and pride is not easily eliminated. Parents need to prayerfully work on their motivational challenges consistently and patiently.

QUESTIONS & ANSWERS

Q How can you be patient and long-suffering when the child is so difficult to deal with?

A Some adult children can really be a pain. Some are even criminal and abusive. The Lord doesn't expect us to give an adult child everything he or she wants, nor does He expect us to ignore offensive behavior. Caring for and blessing our children sometimes requires that we do some very hard things. If you stay close to the Lord and seek inspiration about what you should do, you will be guided in how to deal with the difficult child. The key here is your own motivation, and that will dictate the tone of your actions. If that motivation is love, you will be in control and have peace, even though your adult child may not like what you are doing.

Q I have a son that is not doing what he should be doing. My father (his grandfather) is really concerned and has been zealous in trying to get him to change. He thinks we are too soft on our son. I am afraid that what my dad is doing will push my son further away from us and from the Church. What can I do?

A Ask your father to back off. You should be willing to listen to his counsel, but his direct involvement with your son should come at either your or your son's request. It is not the "program" to push children away through our harshness or condemnation. We can be kind and gentle and at the same time clearly nonaccepting of unacceptable behavior. Sometimes that is a fine balance, but it can be done. If you are going to err, do it on the side of charity and its attributes.

Q When I ask my son what he is doing with his life, he tells me that it is none of my business. He is living with me and not doing well, in my opinion. What is your advice?

A He may be right. If you are asking too much, he really may not need to tell you that much. Since he is living in your home, he has more of an obligation to let you know what's happening with him than if he didn't. But if what he's doing is not negatively affecting you or other children in your home, you may need to let your curiosity about what's happening with him subside. Play this one like one adult dealing with another. Talk to him about your concern and let him respond. Love him.

Q Sure I comment on how dirty my married daughter's bathrooms are. These children don't have the same concern over cleanliness that I have, and I can't seem to get that concern across other than by telling her. What's wrong with that?

A Much of what is wrong with that is the way you tell her. To be in a crowded house and say something like, "These children just don't keep house like we did," is a pretty cruel thing to say. We have a tendency to forget what it was like to have little children, don't we? In any case, we ought to be more concerned about constructively helping to change an undesirable condition, rather than forcing the change through intimidation and harping. Maybe you would see some progress if you offered to help when you are there rather than talking about it so much. Work at solving the problem, not making it worse.

Q How can we get our son to go on a mission? He was planning on it all of his life, and now he has a girlfriend he's getting thick with and doesn't know whether he's going to go or not. We ask him about it all of the time and tell him he needs to stop getting serious with this girl, but he doesn't listen.

A Sometimes the anxiety of parents causes them to do and say things that have exactly the opposite effect on their children than what they want. Maybe you have said enough. Your son knows how you feel, and he probably knows he should go on a mission. To continue to say it can be construed by your son as criticism and might begin to turn him off from any counsel you offer. Maybe you should try something like this: sit down with your son and tell him why you want him to go on a mission so badly. Express your love to him and acknowledge that you have probably pushed too hard and ask him to forgive you. Let him know that this is his decision to make and ask him to ask the Lord for help in making it. Tell him that you will try very hard not to bug him about this anymore but that he needs to understand it will be on your minds because you love him. Invite him to talk to you about it when he is ready. Then pray for him day and night as you are already doing. That's not a sure formula to get him on a mission, but you probably won't lose your son.

Q What about protecting our family's reputation? If any of my children do things that give us a bad name, they're going to be out of here! And they know it. I think each child has a responsibility to the family, and if he or she doesn't want to accept that, then he or she isn't part of the family anymore.

A Each person makes his or her own reputation, and it shouldn't depend on what someone else in the family does or doesn't do. Of course, all of us hope our children have enough love for our family that they will consider how their actions may hurt the family. But that awareness usually takes some time to develop. In the meantime, we need to be concerned about our own motives in dealing with our children. Love-inspired tough responses to our children's actions are usually okay. Prideful tough responses usually aren't. You may want to take a close look at your own motives before you act in such a harsh way.

CHAPTER 5

GROWING UP IS HARD TO DO

Principle 5: Appropriate parental flexibility and patience enhance the "growing-up" process.

A story is told of Camilla Kimball, wife of President Spencer W. Kimball. After a talk she gave to an audience of young women, one young sister came up to her and asked, "How did you ever get to marry a prophet?" Sister Kimball purportedly replied, "He wasn't a prophet when I married him." Prophets aren't prophets right out of the chute. They *become* prophets through life's experiences and what they do with those experiences.

Sometimes parents expect to see the finished product in their children way before the perfecting process is completed. They forget that it takes time. Lots of it. Other than Jesus Christ, no one has lived perfectly as a child or as an adult. One reason for this is that only the Savior had a perfect Father and a nearly perfect mother. How can a child know what perfect is? That is a humbling thought for us parents, isn't it?

Of course, what this says about the need for parental patience and flexibility with our adult children is obvious. We are all still on this perfecting journey, and parents are just slightly ahead of their children (or at least should be) in this trek. We need to share with them what we have learned and be aware that they haven't yet seen, heard, and felt what we have. We also need to understand that all of us have our own progression clock. We all don't experience and learn the same things at the same time. The parents in the following story are a good example of allowing children to progress at their own speed.

Wayne and Carlene were more than frustrated with their son Jared. He was a good young man who went to church but seemed to be living at a maturity level years younger than he was. The time came and passed for him to go on a mission. It didn't bother Jared. He idolized Elvis Presley and wanted to remain a teenager. He combed his hair like Elvis, talked like Elvis, and spent hours in his room with his guitar trying to sing like Elvis. He never came close to sounding like Elvis, but he did get pretty good on the guitar. This went on for years. All of Jared's friends were teenagers even when he was in his late twenties. Wayne and Carlene did everything they knew how to do, then finally were just satisfied with wearing earplugs when Jared sang. They went on with their lives, because Jared had a job, paid his way, and didn't cause any trouble. They hoped that he would grow out of it someday. For a long time it didn't seem like he would, but he finally did. He got married, now has children, and has even served in a bishopric. Their patience paid off. (He still likes Elvis, but he *loves* his parents.)

Parents' expectations of their adult children need to be realistic. Understanding that our life's journey is also a perfecting process fosters patience in our children's progress. Parents should give their adult children ample time to mature, and help them through that process.

SEASONS

When Dan's son Nathan was eighteen, they had a somewhat heated discussion. Nathan turned to his father and asked him incredulously, "Are you sure you want me to do that?"

Dan replied, "I have no idea if I'm right or wrong. I've never been the father of an eighteen-year-old before, and I'm doing the best I know how to do."

It was Nathan's turn. "And I've never been eighteen before, and I'm doing the best I know how to do." That broke the ice between father and son. They both backed off, and their challenge was resolved.

Life is a series of phases or seasons—seasons that, by definition, we have never been through before and will not go through again. We are all plowing new ground constantly, both as parents and adults. By understanding the reality of seasons through adult life, we can make the adjustments that are inevitable with season changes more meaningful and less stressful.

There is considerable opinion as to what constitutes such seasons. Some describe life's seasons as stages of physical, mental, and emotional ability, while others define seasons in terms of relationships, spiritual awareness, faith, or love. Many talk about occupational, educational, or economic phases of life as well. Life seasons or phases, whatever they may be, are age driven and chronological. Furthermore, they overlap without clear demarcation between them and bring special challenges that need to be taken into account in any parent–adult child relationship. These challenges include the following:

- Most adults tend to approach significant changes in their life's seasons with apprehension.
- What is acceptable behavior in one of life's seasons may not be in another.
- Entry into and passage out of a life-season do not come at the same time for everyone.
- People often do better in some phases of life than they do in others.
- Almost all adults do better after they are well into a particular season of their life than they do at its beginning.
- For parents and their adult children, life's seasons often change concurrently.

Parents who deal successfully with their adult children are mindful that seasons define life, and they recognize the inherent challenges that come with these seasons. They adjust their expectations for their children accordingly.

TIMES ARE CHANGING

An overriding condition that plays a critical role in parent–adult child relationships is the constancy and rapidity of societal change. Consider this next story an illustration of how quickly society changes.

A few years ago, Ben, a student in the fourth grade, took his great-grandfather Will for show-and-tell to his grade school class. Will was born in the early 1890s, years before the Wright Brothers flew the first plane. He was raised in a small farming community in southeastern Idaho and was a teenager before he saw his first automobile. He attended a red one-room schoolhouse with children of different ages in the same class. He rode his horse to school and was barefoot when the weather permitted. There wasn't cold or hot running water in his home, and the privy was located a safe distance behind the house. His clothes were made by his mother and were washed out by hand. Presents were usually handmade. Kerosene lamps provided lighting in the home, and his entertainment came in the form of hunting, fishing, and reading, as well as family, church, and community socials. Diseases were rampant, effective medicine virtually nonexistent, and midwives usually delivered the babies at home. Will's mother cooked the meals, tended the house, and raised the children. His father was gone from dawn to dusk working his small farm. When people were in love, they got married and had children—in that order.

The young students he spoke to lived a vastly different life than he had when he was young. They were being raised on computers, fast-food dinners, and a steady diet of TV and movie violence, immorality, and sensory extravagance. Men on the moon and exploration of distant planets were history. Mom and Dad both worked, and most homes had conveniences not even dreamed of in Will's day. Most moms didn't know how to sew, and many did not cook. Virtually all of the children had flown on an airplane, knew what abortion was, and took a shower daily. There were children of various colors and backgrounds in the class, all seeming to look at each other as equals. America had not been to war since they were born, and they had little idea what it meant to be patriotic.

The class spent over an hour asking Will questions about what it was like when he was a boy, completely dumbfounded that what was a normal part of the life of every child today didn't even exist when this man was young. The social, economic, religious, and technological changes that occurred over Will's lifetime were staggering. As a boy he would not have anticipated or been able to keep up with them.

We apparently have not seen anything yet. Change seems to be occurring at an ever-accelerating rate. Wise parents will recognize that things are not today what they were when they were growing up. And they will not be tomorrow what they are today. While fundamental principles of morality, integrity, and charity still apply, the context under which we now operate has changed and will continue to change dramatically. That, in turn, brings about changes in the way people do things and think about things. If parents are not flexible in their relationships with their children as a result, those relationships may needlessly be damaged.

ADAPTING AND COMPROMISING

How do you know when to be flexible? How do you know under what conditions you should be willing to compromise? How do you know when to even be involved with your adult children's decisions? Sorry, but there are no pat answers here. The best we can do is to tell you that most of the time you will *feel* what is right to do if you have genuine concern for your children and have an attitude of flexibility and compromise. Here are three examples showing how parents handled situations at various "seasons" of their children's lives.

Example 1: When the line between being an adult and being a child is wavy and fuzzy. Harry is eighteen. He wants to borrow the family Jeep to go camping next weekend with three of his male friends. The activity is a good one and sounds fun to Dad. Dad trusts Harry a lot. He knows he will take good care of himself, the Jeep, and his friends. Dad teaches Harry for a minute, letting him know about some possible pitfalls, and then agrees to let him take the Jeep on the outing.

A day later, Harry comes to Dad and says some things have changed about the camping trip. Some other friends want to go. They are girls, and they will be camping separately in another area. Dad has confidence in his son, his friends, and these girls. They will handle themselves appropriately, he feels. Dad is concerned about the mixed group camping together, but he agrees Harry can still take the Jeep.

Later in the day Harry comes to Dad again. Another friend, a guy, and the guy's girlfriend are going along. Dad doesn't trust these two, and the whole situation changes. Dad is really concerned. He thinks this camping trip could develop into something more than just camping, and he doesn't want Harry to go or to allow his Jeep to be used. He tells Harry the trip has just turned into a bad idea.

Dad tells Harry that he doesn't want him to go, but he really can't keep him from going. He tells Harry he can take the Jeep if he will go back to the original plan of just the four boys going, but under no other condition. If Harry goes with the girls and the guy and his girlfriend, he will go against Dad's will and will have to use someone else's car. Dad worries about this all night, and the next morning he wakes up knowing that no matter what the boys say they will do, the girls will be there along with the fifth boy and his girlfriend. He decides now he doesn't want Harry up there under any condition and rescinds his offer to let Harry take the Jeep, period.

Harry is not happy and decides to go on the trip anyway. They travel in the family car of one of Harry's friends. The girls go too. The fifth boy and girl go, but do not stay since the group doesn't let them party the way they want to. Everything goes well, and Harry and his friends have a good time. Dad is a little sorry he rescinded his decision to let Harry take the Jeep.

Harry comes to Dad a month later with the same request to borrow the Jeep. Dad lets him take the Jeep without any further discussion.

Becoming an adult is a process, not an event. Parents need to adjust their levels of trust and, in some instances, even their rules, to reflect their children's progress toward adulthood.

Example 2: When adult children make their first critical life decisions. Dennis looks forward to the marriage of his children. As much as he enjoys the teenage years of his children, he spends a lot of time eagerly thinking about whom they will marry, how those marriages will affect their lives, and how much he would enjoy being involved with these new members of his family. Then it happens.

His oldest son, Sam, serves a mission, comes home, and finds a young woman he likes a lot. He courts her, then brings her home one evening to announce to the family that he has asked her to marry him. Dennis is concerned. She doesn't fit his image of Sam's wife. He just knows this is not the woman for his son.

Dennis tells Sam this and says he ought to think long and hard before he goes through with this marriage. Sam assures his father that this young woman is the right one, but he will consider what his dad has told him. Dennis continues to try to convince Sam not to marry the girl until finally Sam asks him to stop. Sam and the young woman are married, and everything turns out very well.

Dennis realizes that Sam has followed all of the counsel that he and his wife have given him about selecting a mate. Sam has chosen carefully and wisely, and the decision was his, not Dennis's or his wife's.

When their children are younger, parents take a very active, if not deciding, role in important decisions their children make. As the children become adults, parental involvement in their decisions should become more and more limited to counseling only. There comes a time when adult children *will* make their own decisions, regardless of what Mom and Dad think or want them to do. Wise parents sense that time and back off accordingly.

Example 3: When adult children have their own families. Marianne loves her grandchildren and feels that her daughters are being good mothers to them. Her daughter Rachel, however, is very tolerant of her five-year-old son's abusive behavior. He often shouts at his mother and sometimes slaps her. He shouts at Marianne and her husband too. Rachel usually just ignores it or even laughs at it. Marianne is concerned about the harmful effects of this developing habit, but she has kept her feelings to herself, hoping that the situation will work itself out.

After thinking about it, she finally decides that she will not say anything about it if it occurs in Rachel's home, but if her grandson is abusive in her home, she will say something. The next time Rachel and her children visit Marianne's home, the five-year-old is abusive to both his mother and his grandmother. Marianne speaks to Rachel and tells her that she feels the boy's behavior is not acceptable and that it is offensive to her and to others. She tells her that it is her opinion that if the behavior is allowed to continue without being checked, the boy will have great difficulties when he starts school. She goes on to say that this is her home and that although she loves her grandson, she does not want to tolerate that kind of behavior there. She asks Rachel if she will control him, at least when he is in her home.

At first Rachel is defensive of her son's behavior, but after thinking about it for a while, she and her husband decide that they need to do something, and they begin to implement consequences whenever the abusive behavior occurs. Her son's behavior improves markedly.

Sometime later Rachel talks to a friend. They discuss the way their own parents are involved in their lives. Rachel says that her parents rarely involve themselves in the affairs of her family, so when they do, she knows that what they say is usually worth heeding.

The older and more independent adult children become, the less parents should give direct, unsolicited counsel. When they do, it should be concerning an important matter and should be well thought out, rather than reactive. The relationship between parents and their adult children will vary according to the child and the circumstances. It is dynamic rather than static. That relationship also changes with age and maturity. Parents should adapt their involvement accordingly.

KEEPING DOORS UNLOCKED

Sometimes when adult children seem to be really out of hand, parents wonder if they should be involved at all in their children's lives. Some parents may even want to be relieved of further burden or strain by absolving themselves of any more responsibility (or even contact) with their problem children. They not only would take their children into the dark woods and leave them, but would send birds out to eat any bread crumbs the children had dropped to help them find their way back home again.

Such parents have lost, or have never had, an eternal perspective. Such parents are not doing all that they can or should do to fulfill their sacred obligation to their children. Elder Robert D. Hales, then Presiding Bishop of the Church and now a member of the Quorum of the Twelve Apostles, said, "A child, even one raised with great love and care and carefully taught, may choose, when an adult, not to follow those teachings for a variety of reasons. How should we react? We understand and respect the principle of agency. We pray that life's experiences will help them regain their desire and ability to live the gospel. They are still our children, and we will love and care about them always. We do not lock the doors of our house nor the doors to our heart" ("How Will Our Children Remember Us?" *Ensign,* November 1993, 10).

We need to be patient while our children grow up—spiritually, as well as physically, emotionally, and mentally. We must never, ever give up on them. The Lord can help us; so can others.

USING THE REST OF YOUR TEAM

Parents are not the only ones who have the potential to influence their adult children for good. Mom and Dad can only do so much to assist a child who has reached adulthood. Bishops and other ecclesiastical leaders, members of the immediate and extended family, friends, and professional therapists may also be of help. We have a tendency as parents to hope we can solve all our children's problems by ourselves. In addition, when the issues are particularly sensitive, we are naturally concerned about not letting our challenges with our children become known outside of the immediate family.

Sometimes, though, adult children are hesitant to confide in their parents or to accept their counsel. In other instances, parents simply do not know what to say or do to help a struggling child. When parents are mostly concerned about the well-being of their children, they will be willing to get the needed help from other people who are also interested in the welfare of their children.

A bishop we know worked with a relieved family who found that their errant daughter, away at college, decided to repent and return to Church activity. The parents had prayed and fasted for her well-being for a long time. The bishop felt the Spirit guiding him as he worked with her. In time, she prepared for a temple marriage. There was joy at her wedding reception when her father met the bishop for the first time. "It's great to meet another member of the team," were his first words to the bishop. "Thank you for what you have done for our daughter."

Parents can provide only part of the total support needed by their children throughout their lives. Wise parents recognize this and actively seek assistance from and coordinate with the other members of the team who have as a common interest the well-being of their children.

PONDERING THE PRINCIPLE

Parents' relationships with their adult children vary just as they did when the children were young. Not only does each child have his or her own unique personality and way of doing things, but also both the timing and the process of "growing up" differs with each child. The complexity and overlapping of life-seasons and a drastically changing world further complicates those relationships. Most parents more or less muddle through all of this, but wise parents come into it with a willingness to compromise, when necessary, to preserve good relationships as well as to do what is best for their adult children. Importantly, they are also willing to tap into resources outside of the immediate family to help them bless their children.

- Parents' expectations for their adult children need to be tempered according to the uniqueness of each child.
- Life's seasons overlap one another, creating "fuzzy," unpredictable time segments where both parent and adult child behavior are often more inconsistent. In our rapidly changing world, sometimes procedures that used to be effective become ineffective or even counterproductive.
- While there is no exact formula for dealing with adult children in this very complex world, parents who have a real concern for their children will often be prompted as to what is right for them to do.
- Parents who patiently keep doors open for even the most errant adult child are following the example of Heavenly Father.
- There is a team of concerned individuals whose efforts to assist challenged adult children are made more effective as parents recognize and utilize them.

The fruits of an *adaptation attitude* on the part of parents with adult children are patience and compassion, with a high likelihood that more than acceptable parent–adult child relationships and positive outcomes will result.

QUESTIONS & ANSWERS

Q My adult children do not come to reunions. What are we doing wrong?

A Probably nothing. Just remember that what is enjoyable to you, such as conversing with relatives you have known for decades, discussing family history, and reminiscing, is not usually all that much fun for young adults. Reunions take substantial time if both husband and wife have families that hold lots of reunions. One young couple we know had reunions for eight weekends during the summer they were first married. That's eight weekends spent where one of the spouses didn't know the people he or she was visiting with. Of course, family reunions are a good thing, generally. You might try asking your children what it would take to get them to come. Put them in charge of some part they would enjoy, and try to make the reunions more exciting. Remember that they may have "real" excuses, like the expenses involved or their vacation schedule. Keep inviting them, but understand if they don't come.

Q My children are choosing some very strange names for their children and are moving away from our family traditions. How can I convince them to be more traditional in name selection? Our family has always used the old names, and I want them to keep this important family tradition.

A Quit worrying about it. Since this is so important to you, speak about it to your children before the child is born and then let it go. You could worry about this one for the rest of your life, but it isn't worth it.

Q We have a thirty-one-year-old single son who has walked away from at least three potential wives at different times in his life. He is always worried that there might be a better one around the corner and is afraid to make a decision. How can we help him with this decision?

A There may not be a lot you can do. One thing you shouldn't do is be hard on him and nag. There is probably no one who is more frustrated with his situation than he is, so give him your trust and support. Remember, not everyone becomes emotionally ready for marriage in his or her twenties, so don't push too hard. On the other hand, if you feel his anxieties here are really abnormal, you might suggest some counseling, either with his bishop or a professional counselor. Be careful in how you suggest this, though. It is probably important that the counselor he sees be LDS, since non-LDS counselors often have much different opinions about marriage.

Q I know that we can put too much pressure on our children when we expect too much of them, but can't we expect too little as well?

A Certainly. We should never stop encouraging; we should just stop nagging. It is not wrong for parents to express their *reasonable* expectations to their children and to encourage them toward those expectations. The problems come when this *reasonable* expectation becomes a fixation with the parents or when their expectations are not reasonable. When either one of these things happens, relationships are going to suffer.

Q I have invested much more money in my adult children than my parents ever invested in me. Am I going about this all wrong?

A Remember, times have changed since you first started out. You probably were able to get into your first home not too long after your marriage because the down payment was low and your monthly payment wasn't much different than what you were paying for rent. Chances are you didn't need help from your parents. The same probably held true for buying a car and other major purchases. It's also a good bet that your parents didn't have "extra" money like you do today, and it wasn't really a choice for them whether to give much to their adult children. The criteria you should use here is not what your parents did or did not do, but whether or not *you* think what you are giving (or are contemplating giving) your children will help them. If you think it has helped, then don't worry about it. If you think it will help and if you can afford to do it, then go ahead. A word of caution: There is a wide difference of opinion about what parents should be willing to give their children. Sometimes the worst thing is to give too much and keep your children from having some valuable experience with "struggle." As a general rule, though, err on the side of generosity. Try to evaluate each situation by the Spirit, and you won't go far wrong.

Q We are proud of our married children and like to have them go with us to our business and social events, but they don't seem to like to go with us all that much. My wife and I feel really bad about that. Should we just stop inviting them or tell them how we feel about it or what? We don't want to cause bad feelings.

A You should be considerate of your children and their time. You might try to be more selective in what you invite them to—events you think they might especially enjoy. Invite them in a way that they won't feel guilty if they say no. For example, you might explain what is going to take place at the event and ask them if that would be something they would like to go to. If it is, invite them. If it isn't, don't. Remember, they have their lives to live too.

Q My children have spoken about having children soon after they get married. How do I convince them that they should wait until they get their education before having children?

A You're not going to get the answer you want from us. First of all, that is their decision. It's between them and the Lord, and you need to let them make it. What you can do is to counsel them to listen to what the Church leaders have said (their counsel is to not postpone having a family if at all possible); take a look at their financial, physical, and emotional circumstances; and seek the Spirit for guidance. You'll get yourself in a peck of trouble pushing them in a direction that is contrary to priesthood counsel and their own spiritual feelings.

Q When we have family gatherings at our house, we often tell our children to leave their younger ones at home. We have a very nice house, and some of our grandchildren are really destructive. I know that some of our children resent this, but I don't want our home wrecked. What should I do?

A This is a serious problem from both sides. It is wrong for your children to allow their children to run unsupervised through your home. You have a right to have nice things and to keep them "safe." On the other hand, it is natural for parents to bristle when Grandma tells them to leave some of their children home when they come to her house. The answer here is *compromise*. Sit down with your adult children and explain your concerns. Ask them to be mindful of their children when they are at your house. You might consider having "off-limits" rooms when they come over and center your activities in rooms that you have childproofed. It is the parents' responsibility to keep their younger ones out of the "off-limits" rooms. Hold them to it. If necessary, buy small locks for the doors and place them out of reach of the smaller children. You should be tolerant of a little inconsequential breakage or wall scuffs. Have your adults-only family gatherings, but make most of your family activities for all of the family. It will pay in the long run.

Q Do we really have to be all that careful about what we say and do with one another? Aren't we all family, and shouldn't we be able to have some latitude in these things?

A We are all family, and maybe that is the reason we ought to be careful about what we say and do. Those we love the most have the power to hurt us the most. The reverse is also true. If we really love, we should want to do everything possible to help and bless those we love rather than saying or doing things that could cause pain and sorrow. Be careful what you say and do to your family members *because* you love them.

Q When each of my eight children was born, my mother came and stayed with me for several weeks to help me get on my feet. I want to do that with my daughters too because it meant so much to me. Some of them seem to like me to do this, but with others I feel like I am interfering. Any suggestions?

A What a wonderful mother you had! Remember, though, you *wanted* her there. You should express to your daughters how meaningful your experience was with your mother and let them know that you would like to do that with each of them, but tell them that is their choice. Don't make them feel bad if they don't want you to do it. Some couples like to share that sacred time by themselves without anyone else around, and that's okay. Offer your service, but don't push it on them.

Q When do you know whether or not you should get some outside professional help when you are having traumatic struggles with one of your children?

A When it is apparent that the problem your child is having is beyond your ability to handle. Get help when you have done what you *reasonably feel* you can and should do and the situation doesn't change markedly. Your bishop or priesthood or Relief Society leader is a good place to start.

Q What should I do when my adult child refuses to listen to me or to any other good person when they are in trouble?

A Try to get some peace of mind for yourself. Your team is not just for your child, but for you as well. Use them to help give you ideas and, more important, comfort.

CHAPTER 6

WHY ASK THE "WHY" QUESTION?

Principle 6: Our time is usually best spent looking for solutions to challenges rather than for who is to blame.

In many instances, it is unlikely that we can ever know all of the causes or even the most significant factors for the challenging behavior of some of our adult children. Therefore, it is often counter-productive to focus our energies on trying to determine the "whys" rather than concentrating on what we are going to do about the challenges we are now facing.

PREOCCUPATION WITH GUILT

Some parents become consumed with trying to determine why their adult children are having serious problems. They succumb to the natural tendency to blame themselves, with its resulting energy-sucking self-flagellation. While all parents fall short (remember, we are learning too), there are few who have not raised their children the best that they could, given the unique circumstances they faced and knowing what they knew at the time. Of course, it is right for parents to be introspective and to repent as they see things in their own lives that need to be changed. It is not right to become preoccupied with the "what-might-have-beens," thus denying troubled adult children the kind of parental attention and focus that could really help them now. The couple in the next story soon realized that focusing on their past "mistakes" was not helping their children deal with their current problems.

Ted and Marie Landrau have been married nearly thirty years. This is the second marriage for both. Marie's first marriage ended in divorce a few months after the birth of her first baby. She was not a member of the Church at the time and was baptized shortly after the divorce. Ted, on the other hand, is a lifelong member of the Church and married in the temple. He and his first wife had had three children when she decided to leave him and leave the Church. The children were all very young and stayed with Ted, as their mother didn't want anything to do with them. Ted and Marie met and were married, combining their young children into one family.

One additional child was born to them, making five children in all. They were very active in the Church and raised their children the best they knew how. They loved them and expressed that love outwardly and consistently. But as each child grew to become a teenager and then an adult, severe problems developed with virtually every one. One son got a young woman pregnant, then married her. Another son had consistent challenges with the law, while another one became actively homosexual and left the Church. The two daughters did not fare much better. They both became inactive and married outside the Church to men who were abusive. Their lives were miserable until they finally divorced.

As the first of their children began to give them challenges, Ted and Marie spent many sleepless nights wondering what they could have done differently. They saw plenty of things that they felt they should have done or shouldn't have done. They wondered if their own earlier lives before their marriage had contributed to what was now happening with their children. They were consumed with guilt.

Over time, however, they came to the realization that they had done the best they knew how and that it didn't do anyone any good to fret about the past. As they began to focus their attention on what they might be doing now to help the children, they started to feel some peace in their lives. They still wonder about the "whys" of all of this from time to time (you can't really stop that), but it is no longer distracting them. They are happier now, and their decisions relative to their children have started to bring about some positive results.

PLACING THE BLAME WHERE IT USUALLY DOESN'T BELONG

Another problem that can occur when parents are unwisely absorbed with the "why" question is that the blame is misplaced. Since there is hardly ever a simple reason why an adult child's behavior is what it is, parents become frustrated with their inability to zero in on *the* answer. The tendency, then, is for them to simplify by seeking a scapegoat. That uncomplicates everything, and the parents begin to focus on that one thing. As often as not, that one thing is someone or something other than their child.

For example, we have heard numerous versions of the following scapegoats:

- "If our son's wife had just been more sensitive to his needs, he would have been faithful to her."
- "Our daughter's problems started when she began going around with these friends of hers. They make her act different than she really is."
- "Our son's bishop has driven him from the Church."
- "I am always making my daughter angry. I continually say or do the wrong thing, and if I would just change she would like me better."
- "Our son's bosses are all money driven and don't want anyone around them who is more interested in what's best for people, so he keeps losing his job."
- "If our daughter's husband would just honor his priesthood, our daughter would come around too and be a better mother."

And on and on.

In virtually every one of these cases, the adult children are let off the hook. They are not being held accountable for their actions; hence, their actions will probably continue. In the meantime, the parents agonize in unwarranted self-blame or in debilitating hatred or dislike for someone or something that is beyond their ability to control. So their adult child's behavior goes unchanged, and their own misery and frustration continues.

WHEN ANSWERING THE "WHY" QUESTION CAN BE HELPFUL

Obviously, knowing the most significant causes of an adult child's problem can help lead to solutions to the problem. Sometimes, we can even see clearly what those causes are. What we must strive to avoid is becoming so caught up in the "whys" that we don't effectively deal with our current challenges. In general, parents should be concerned with "why" when it is reasonably clear they can do something with that knowledge to help their adult children now or in the future. Here are two examples.

Sharpening the focus. With the limited resources (including time and energy) that are available to any parents, making the most efficient use of those resources just makes sense. Knowing what is likely causing the adult child's problem allows parents to do this. They get to use the rifle rather than the shotgun in trying to do something about it. A classic instance here would be when it is determined that the child has abnormal physiological, mental, or emotional challenges. Rather than trying to deal with the problem on their own with "standard" parenting techniques, parents can bring in the professional help that is really necessary to effectively handle it.

Making appropriate changes. Sometimes it *is* the parents' fault, or at least they are a significant part of the problem. Parents are not going to change until they know that what they are doing (or not doing) is a major cause of the problem with their adult child. Knowing that what they are doing *now* is part of the problem allows parents to make the kinds of changes in their own lives that will help their children. However, they should not dwell on their uncorrectable actions that happened years ago. They should be satisfied with acknowledging those weaknesses, then get on with their lives.

PONDERING THE PRINCIPLE

Energy and time are limited resources. Parents dealing with challenging adult children need to strive to use these resources in the most efficient and effective way they can. Usually this means they should concentrate their efforts on doing what they can do today to help alleviate those challenges, rather than squandering scarce resources on fruitless finger-pointing and faultfinding expeditions into the past. Sometimes, however, it is possible to determine causes of adult children problems with relative clarity. When that knowledge can be helpful in dealing effectively with those problems, parents need to seek it and use it.

- Parents should never let their concern about the causes of an adult child's challenging behavior get in the way of trying to do something about those challenges.
- Parent preoccupation with "what-might-have-beens" is usually counterproductive.
- Parents obsessed with determining causes of the unsatisfactory behavior of their adult children are inclined to place the blame where it doesn't belong.
- Parents should focus on the "why" question only when it is virtually certain that this knowledge will help them better assist their adult children.

If parents will focus on doing what will most help their adult children who are having special challenges, they can avoid being distracted by unanswerable questions about the cause. The results will often be positive in helping adult children overcome their problems and nearly always will bring about more peace of mind for the parents.

QUESTIONS & ANSWERS

Q Our daughter has just informed us that she has been convicted of a crime that occurred over a year ago and that she has been sentenced to 120 days in jail with her sentence beginning in a few weeks. She claims she is innocent and that the lawyer she had was really bad and didn't try hard enough. She has spoken to another attorney who thinks she got a raw deal and says he can do something about it. But he wants one thousand dollars up front. Our daughter doesn't have the money and has asked us for a loan. She has been in trouble all of her adult life, but over the last five or six months seems to be making some progress. She has three grade-school-age children at home and just recently remarried. Her husband works construction and has sporadic employment. We don't know whether she is innocent or not, and we don't want to enable her if she's guilty. What should we do?

A   In this case you should be more concerned with what will happen to the children if your daughter goes to jail than with what caused her present situation. We suggest you first find out if the attorney she wants to represent her is reputable. If he is, tell your daughter to allow him to divulge everything to you that you want, then give him a call. Have him go over with you what he thinks he can do for your daughter and why he feels it will work. If you are satisfied that there is a reasonable chance that he can do something, you probably should agree to help if you can afford it. If she goes to jail, the time that you spend and the expenses that you incur to help the children, if they *can* be helped, will probably be much greater than what you would have spent on attorney's fees. You should tell your daughter this is a loan and have her sign an agreement to pay it back systematically over a reasonable time.

Q   I don't think anybody has the problems with their adult children that I do—at least I haven't talked to anyone who does. It's got to be my fault when they've all turned out so poorly, but I don't know what to do about it. My children think it's my fault too and remind me about it all the time. I have been single since my children were teenagers, and I know that's had something to do with it too. I am so depressed about all of this that sometimes I can't even function. What can I do now to help them?

A   For one thing, don't let them get away with slapping the blame for their own misconduct on you. You raised them under very difficult circumstances and probably did the best you could. The best thing you can do now is to stop beating yourself and get on with your own life. Don't excuse their unacceptable behavior, but continue to love them. They are making the choices to do what they are doing, and that likely has nothing to do with what you are doing or probably what you did. They will find that out in time.

Q Our thirty-year-old son was arrested for embezzlement. He wasn't sent to jail but is paying his employers back. He is very bitter about it because he claims his employers were not paying him what he deserved and they owed him the money anyway. I think he's got a point, but I don't think it was right to take the money either. I don't know what to tell him when he brings this up. What do you suggest? (He brings it up all of the time.)

A Your son has a problem, and it has nothing to do with his former employers. You probably heard him say when he was in school that he got an unacceptable grade because his teacher was bad. Your son's problem is a lack of honesty, primarily with himself. Until he's willing to accept responsibility for his dishonesty rather than blaming someone else, he's going to continue to get in trouble. Do him a favor and speak straight to him. You are enabling him by saying nothing.

Q Our twenty-two-year-old daughter lives with us and is going to school and working. Her behavior toward us and the rest of the family is barely tolerable (she is critical and verbally abusive). Sometimes, though, she goes for days without saying anything to anybody and then will just blow up. What do you advise that we do?

A Get some professional counsel here from a doctor or psychologist. Her behavior is not normal and will probably not change without some professional help.

Q I don't know what to do with our youngest son. All of our other children were at the top of their class in high school, but he seemed satisfied to just make it through. He did not go to college before his mission and just worked enough to give him spending money. He served a mission, but didn't get called to any leadership positions. People seem to like him, but at the rate he's going he's not going to be an achiever like we want him to be. We've tried about everything from setting goals for him to trying to embarrass him because of what he's doing (or not doing). Nothing has worked so far. In fact, if anything, he seems to be getting worse. Any suggestions?

A Yes. Leave him alone and let him go at his own pace. Encourage him rather than criticize, and compliment him when he makes progress, even if it isn't as much as you want. It is possible that he is reacting against the constant pressure that he feels from you to excel. It may be that he doesn't think he is able to meet your expectations anyway and consequently refuses to try to do much of anything. Of course that is his choice, but never feeling that he is doing anything that is acceptable to his parents can be a pretty imposing barrier. In this case, what you are doing may be having exactly the opposite effect from what you are intending. Step back and take a look, then make the appropriate changes in what you are doing.

CHAPTER 7

LIKE IT OR NOT, YOU'RE PLAYING DOMINOES

Principle 7: Parental decisions regarding any member of the family will affect every other member. Where the family's finite resources are used is usually an either/or choice.

Lon and Emma have raised four sons, who have each gone on missions and married beautiful young women in the temple. Lon has worked hard all of his life and has accumulated enough to ensure a comfortable retirement and to help his sons get into homes. He has been very disciplined about this and has saved just the right amount. Lon and Emma have had a textbook LDS family up until now, but things have changed.

Their oldest son, Fred, is having some very serious problems. A few years back the doctors told him he needed to have an operation if he was to live a normal life. He had let his health insurance lapse, so he had to come up with the money himself. In addition, his wife worked part-time, but could not bring in enough income to support their family of two children while Fred had his operation and was recuperating. They approached Lon and Emma for help.

It turned out they needed over $100,000 for the operation and to help the family get by until Fred was back on his feet. Lon and Emma decided to loan them the money, realizing that they would have to curtail some of their retirement plans. It also meant they could not give as much toward buying homes for their last two children who did not yet own a home. The children without homes supported the decision, even though it would potentially affect them detrimentally.

Now Fred is having deep-seated psychological challenges as well. His wife has been very supportive, but the situation is tenuous. Fred has been receiving psychiatric help for the last two years, with Lon and Emma footing most of those bills. They think if they stop paying for the counseling and medical treatments, Fred will leave his wife and family, and his behavior will ultimately destroy him. He does not seem to be making any progress and is barely holding his own. Fred's needs continue to eat into Lon and Emma's retirement funds and is absorbing their time and concentration as well. The other children and their families do not feel that Lon and Emma spend enough time with them and are very concerned that the retirement years are going to be far less "golden" than Lon and Emma planned for.

Lon and Emma are now seeing that to continue what they are doing will bring serious short- and long-term effects to themselves and their other children.

Like Lon and Emma's response to Fred, our responses (or non-responses) to the actions of an adult child affect to one degree or another everyone in our family. Our resources, including our time, energy, material assets, and emotional or spiritual strength, are limited to the extent that we use them and to the extent that they are gone and therefore not available for use elsewhere. Furthermore, our action or inaction toward one child can generate feelings in our other children that, whether justified or not, are real and need to be recognized.

Since there is almost always a potentially significant domino effect when parents are dealing with an adult child who has challenges, parents should give careful thought to the likely ramifications of their actions on other members of the family. In considering the potential effects of certain actions, conscientious parents also realize that doing nothing is doing something. To put off action is itself a decision and should be considered in light of its effect on all members of the family as well. No one family member should be considered more important than another, and all decisions need to be made with that in mind.

Having said this, we need to give a word of caution. Parents can be so hung up on trying to figure out the extent and content of potential domino effects that nothing is done when something should be. Here are some "don'ts" that can be helpful in avoiding this trap.

- Don't expect to know all potential domino effects. No one can.
- Don't delay making decisions that need to be made just because you can't calculate their absolute effect on other family members.
- Don't quit making important decisions because past domino effects were unsatisfactory.
- Don't expect the domino effect of a second decision to necessarily play itself out the way it did with a first decision (especially if there is a different set of variables).

TREATING ADULT CHILDREN FAIRLY, NOT EQUALLY

Adult children who are going through significant challenges often require more time, attention, and material assistance than children who are not so challenged. For parents to render the *appropriate* amount of aid to adult children with problems, even if it means reducing the resources that would normally be given to other members of the family, does not mean they favor one child over another. Treating adult children *fairly*, not *equally*, is key.

One mother we know was determined to treat each of her adult children exactly equally. From the time she and her husband started to spend money for their children's college educations, she kept track of how much was being given to each child. Over the years, the "real world" changed her view about doing that. Her daughter divorced her abusive husband and needed a great deal of emotional support, as well as help getting on her financial feet. One son's business went sour, and he needed help to keep from losing his home. Her other two children haven't needed any extra help (financial, emotional, or spiritual)—yet. She has stopped her "equality accounting." She and her husband feel they have done the right thing in helping those children who needed the help, while the children who haven't received as much as the others have done well on their own.

Of course, no two adult children are alike, even within the same family. Responsive parents strive to help and support their adult children according to their unique needs. In essence, parental grace should be *sufficient*—not too little and not too much. To do this, even though the total assistance given to each adult child *will be different,* means that parental love for each child is, in fact, the same. Why? Because in a very real sense, the children are all being treated *as equals.* They are getting their needs taken care of when they cannot take care of those needs themselves. It isn't the quantity of the help that counts; it is that the *needed* help is there. Sounds like our Heavenly Father, doesn't it?

UNEQUAL DISTRIBUTION OF RESOURCES— KEEPING IT FAIR

As we have stated, it is important, whenever possible, to consider the potential ramifications on other family members before significantly altering the flow of family resources to an adult child with severe challenges. As often as not, however, parents do not have that luxury, either because of the suddenness of the difficulty or the impossibility of predicting ultimate repercussions. They can only guess what those ramifications will be. In these instances, wise parents will be willing to make the appropriate adjustments in their allocation of scarce resources as the situation plays itself out to make certain that they are dealing fairly with each member of the family, including themselves.

The figure below, sometimes called a Sullivan Circle, depicts a family where everything is going well, with no one adult child needing any more attention than another. In fact, consider it your family. The four quadrants symbolize an equal (or at least "normal") distribution of your resources, including time, energy, and substance, to each of your adult children.

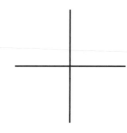

Equal Distribution of Parental Resources

Suddenly, something goes wrong. Your returned-missionary son announces that he has lost his testimony, has been having an affair, and wants to divorce his wife. You panic. You wonder what you have done wrong. You wonder how you can help him and his wife and their children. You wonder how the rest of the children will respond. You wonder how your friends will react when they find out you don't have the model LDS family. You have lots of questions and not many answers. You forget about most everything that is going on around you as you concentrate on this situation. Your Sullivan Circle now looks like this.

Allocated to Challenged Adult Child

Imbalanced Allocation of Parental Resources

The three smaller sections represent the significant diminishing of time, energy, and substance to your other children as this devastating problem with your one child develops. The large segment symbolizes your absorption with your challenged son. His problems have overwhelmed your world. In the short run, you don't know what else to do as you try to come to grips with a serious problem you have never been confronted with before.

However, if you were to continue indefinitely with almost all of your energy and resources focused on your son, you and your family would be in danger of becoming dysfunctional. This not only could impair your and your other children's emotional, spiritual, material, and physical well-being, but also would certainly limit your ability to help your challenged son. You are not being fair to anyone. Appropriate adjustments must be made.

Remember, you are to treat your children fairly, not necessarily equally. When you see that what you are doing detracts from being fair, you need to put forth concerted effort to right matters. That does not mean you need to go back to square one and allocate your scarce resources relatively equally between your children again. Indeed, such an arrangement, given the increased needs of your son, would probably not be fair to him. What you do is put this new situation with your son into perspective (i.e., in the context of your entire family, realizing that each member has his or her own individual needs too), do the best you can, and get on with your life.

For the foreseeable future, that will probably mean your son will continue to receive a disproportionate share of your resources, but not to the overwhelming of the rest of the family. The figure below depicts a normalized condition, with your resources being divided into five segments now, rather than four, and your son, in essence, receiving a double portion for the time being. You are back in control, your situation becomes manageable, and the other members of the family are not being slighted.

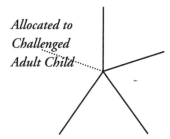

Appropriately Balanced Allocation of Parental Resources

Obviously, putting the family back on a normal track can be a formidable task. However, it can be done, and it should be done. But it will never be done unless parents recognize the need to treat all of their children fairly.

MAKING A PRIORITY OF ASSIGNING PRIORITIES

Parents need to ask themselves two other questions to determine when and where to use their scarce resources in meeting their adult children's needs.

Can we help? It is possible that no matter what parents may do, they are not going to affect the present condition of an adult child in any meaningful way. If they determine, however, that there is something they can do, they should ask themselves a second question.

Can we afford to give the help that is needed? Here, the word *afford* does not refer so much to the amount of resources that are available to use as it does to parent *willingness* to use available resources in any given way. Since the use of any resource to help one child means that that resource will not be available to help another family member (including the parents), parents need to decide who is going to be helped and who is not.

Both of these questions imply the need to prioritize family resources. In fact, whether parents give any thought to this prioritizing or not, prioritization is taking place. It just makes sense to put some thought into it *before* the resource is committed so that the resource is being used in the best way possible. But how do you prioritize correctly? Or, more accurately, how do you prioritize effectively?

That's not an easy question to answer. One thing seems certain, however. Parents are far more likely to make most effective use of their resources when they prayerfully ponder and discuss what they are going to do before they do it. Here are some guidelines that should be helpful.

- Do not use significant resources on highly troubled adult children when the outcome will almost certainly be unacceptable.
- Try to allocate resources in direct proportion to the degree to which positive results are expected.
- Generally, use resources whenever the amount needed is relatively small and the result is likely to prevent an escalation of a minor problem into one that is more severe.

PARENTAL AGREEMENT IS MANDATORY

There is another basic rule of thumb that should be applied when allocating any family resources, including the time and energy of the parents: *Do not use resources for any adult child if they will detrimentally affect husband-wife relationships.*

Spousal bonds are more important than parent–adult child relations. There is a covenant relationship between husband and wife. That moral contract needs to be honored by both spouses and takes precedence over any responsibility to adult children. Unilateral action on the part of one parent without the knowledge or consent of the other will usually be counterproductive with respect to helping the adult child and will almost always create a significant challenge to the marriage itself.

On the other hand, when parents agree on how to allocate resources and work as a team, inspiration and viable ideas on how to best help their adult children are far more likely to be forthcoming. Furthermore, the spiritual and emotional strength that comes with parental unity allows parents both to cope with difficult challenges with their children and to grow as a result of them. Spousal unity and love will prove to be a powerful example to troubled children and be a force, in and of itself, to help the children overcome their problems.

PONDERING THE PRINCIPLE

Since all families have limited resources, including time, energy, and material means, the way any of those resources is allocated will affect every member of the family. Resources that are used to assist one adult child will not be available to help any other member. Furthermore, using or not using resources for any child may cause feelings that can impact the well-being of the individual members of the family and the viability of the family itself. Wise parents should not only be aware of these potential domino effects, but should strive to plan according to the anticipated consequences.

- Doing nothing with respect to a challenged adult child's situation carries with it potential domino effects.
- Parents rarely know all of the possible domino effects and should not let that lack of knowledge keep them from making timely decisions.
- Family resources should be distributed fairly, not necessarily equally, among adult children.

- Parents tend to initially distribute resources unfairly in favor of a challenged adult child and need to make appropriate adjustments as time goes on.
- Making the prioritization of scarce family resources a priority will substantially increase the likelihood of those resources being used in the most effective way.
- Parents need to work together and be considerate of one another when making decisions concerning the use of family resources in helping their adult children.

There are no set formulas for maximizing the effective use of family resources in helping challenged (and not-so-challenged) adult children. However, parents who strive to understand the ramifications of their resource allocation decisions and work to establish some reasonable priorities in making those decisions are more likely to be successful than those who do not.

QUESTIONS & ANSWERS

Q Do we have to have our daughter and her live-in boyfriend over for Thanksgiving when we have invited all of our other adult children and their kids? We all feel so uncomfortable when we are around them.

A No, you don't. It isn't fair to you or to your other children to ruin your Thanksgiving. Invite your daughter to come, but ask her to come by herself. She understands your discomfort with her situation (or should) and will need to make the decision whether to be with you or not.

Q I am widowed and have one adult child who really needs some financial help, but my other children have warned me that it isn't fair if I give more to the one without giving equal amounts to the others. I can afford to help the one, but I cannot afford to do the same for the others. What do you think I should do?

A Call your family together. Tell them that you love them equally and that means that as their mother you have the responsibility to help each one according to his or her needs and your ability to help. That's the way Heavenly Father does it. Tell them that you consider your resources as belonging to Heavenly Father and that you have a responsibility to use those resources as He would. Ask them to allow you to do this as you are inspired to do and to try to understand the principle here. Then proceed as you feel impressed to do. However, what you also should consider doing is spending additional time with the children who may not be getting much in the way of material gifts from you. There are many ways to show your love.

Q We have ten adult children. How can we spend adequate time and resources on each of them? We don't have a lot of either.

A Do the best you can. They know of your limitations and will understand. Prioritize your time and resources according to who needs the help. You might want to consider developing a family fund, where all of your children are invited to contribute as much as they comfortably can. As parents, you would make the decisions as to where those funds were allocated, based on the needs of family members. Try to hold lots of family gatherings as well, then conscientiously strive to spend meaningful time with each person at those functions.

Q I hear what you are saying about treating your adult children fairly rather than equally, but how do you know what is fair?

A You're not going to find any formula for that. But in deciding, if you first have counseled with all of your adult children to get their input, if you have talked with others outside the family who may have been in a situation similar to yours, if you and your spouse have prayed for help and you are in basic agreement about what to do, then you have done all that you can do. Make your decisions and go with them. If you don't feel right about what is happening after a while, then modify what you are doing. Understanding children will not judge you harshly if you are a little out of balance in your fairness, and non-understanding children are probably not going to be happy unless you are biased in favor of them.

Q What would you suggest if your adult children keep track of everything you give any of your other children or grandchildren and remind you when you haven't spent exactly the same amount of time or money with each one, especially with them?

A You don't measure your children's love for you based upon the time and money they spend on you in relationship to that which their siblings are spending on you, and they shouldn't measure your love for them that way either. Explain this to your children and tell them that your resources don't belong to them, just as their resources don't belong to you. You have a right to use your resources as you see fit, as do they. Ask them to put away their ledgers. Tell them to feel free to come to you if they have a need, but not to ever use the excuse that they deserve something more from you than they are getting just because someone else in the family got something they didn't.

Q I have two daughters who want Grandma's antique piano. One of the girls has a nice piano. The other doesn't. They both play well, and they both want the piano. I think the one who doesn't have a nice piano should have it, but the other won't hear of it. She says it isn't fair that she won't get the piano just because she went out and bought a nice piano on her own. What should I do?

A This is your decision to make, not your daughters'. You should call your daughters together to talk about it and tell them that you also have options other than giving the piano to either one. Here a few of them: (1) Put the piano up for sale and give them the first option to buy. If they both want it for your price, have them bid on it or draw straws. If neither one can come up with the money (cash), you can sell the piano and split the money between them. (2) Give the piano to a museum or another family member or friend. (3) If you decide to give it to one of your daughters, let both know that the decision is yours and you have not been swayed by either one of them and you don't want them to fight with each other about it. If you feel you need to do something for the one who doesn't get the piano, then do it. That could be a gift of another family heirloom, or even cash. Make the decision and live with it.

Q My oldest daughter lives in another state and has five children. Four months ago her middle daughter was diagnosed with terminal bone cancer. She has to be driven to the doctor's office several times a week for treatment and diagnosis and requires constant care at home. I have been staying with them for the last three months to help out. (I have not gone home during that time, although my husband flew out a month ago for a few days.) My granddaughter is holding her own, so we could be in for a long siege. My husband and my two other children at home think I ought to go back home now. My daughter says she will be okay with her older children helping out along with the sisters in the ward, but I think I should stay longer. I don't want to leave when I know it will put greater demands on them than they already have. Any advice?

A You have done what you needed to do as this emergency developed, but maybe it's time to start getting back to normal (whatever that is). You didn't say how old your children at home were, but regardless of their age, they need a mother too—and your husband needs a wife. It may be that your daughter and her husband need a little private space too. If you can afford it, you might want to consider going home and flying out to your daughter's once a month for a week or so. These decisions need to be made jointly with your husband. In any event, you probably should consider going home now and keeping a close eye on the situation. If necessary, you might encourage your daughter to bring in a housekeeper periodically. You can offer to help pay for that.

Q We have one major, major problem with our oldest son and a minor problem with our youngest adult son, and we can't help them both. Over the years our oldest son has been in and out of jail, and we have spent a small fortune on him for drug rehab and attorney's fees. He has been accused of doing something really bad this time (armed robbery) and is faced with years in the state penitentiary unless we can get him a good lawyer. That will cost us at least ten thousand dollars. Our youngest son wants to get into a home. He and his wife have been saving for several years, but they are about five thousand short of the down payment they will need and have asked us to help them. They have found a new home they like and are afraid if they wait any longer, the price will go up and they won't be able to afford it. What do you suggest we do?

A   There is an old adage in business: Don't chase good money after bad. Sometimes that applies to the allocation of our resources to our children. While you should never give up hope for a child who has not given you any reason to hope, you should not go on sinking your scarce resources into a bottomless pit, especially when it means you can't share them with your other children who may be in need. Put your younger son and his family into a home and then do the best you can with your older son. Maybe it's time, for his sake, to let him do this one on his own.

Q My wife and I recently married. We both outlived our former spouses. I am retired and only have a get-by retirement income. My wife's deceased husband left her with a large sum of money, though. She has one son who is forty-two years of age, has never been married, and keeps asking her for money. She gives him as much as he wants. I have two married children with large families who are really struggling financially, and I would like to help them, but my wife does not want to use any of her money to do that. What can I do to convince my wife to see she needs to do this?

A   First of all, she doesn't need to help your children. That is her money, and she can do with it as she pleases. If you have tried everything you know to convince her of your children's needs and she still won't respond, you should let it drop. As your marriage grows stronger with time and as she gets to know your children better, she may change the way she feels. Don't push it, though, or you may ruin your marriage.

Q My wife and I do not agree concerning the handling of our adult children. We are at odds for the first time in our marriage. What should we do?

A   First of all, you both need to agree that your own relationship takes precedence over anything you do with your children. If you cannot agree on that principle, then your marriage is in trouble and you will probably need to get some professional counsel. If you can agree, then weigh each potential involvement with your adult children against your spousal relationship. If one of you wants to do something regarding your adult children and the other feels so strongly against it that your relationship will be compromised if it is done, then don't do it. If you are both most concerned about the quality of your marriage, then you should each have a spirit of compromise that will help you get through most disagreements. Sometimes it is also helpful to get a third (or fourth) opinion from someone you both trust and respect—your bishop, for example. Let the Spirit help.

CHAPTER 8

GET A LIFE! (IT'S BETTER THAT WAY)

Principle 8: Choosing to be happy brings peace and increases parents' ability to deal effectively with their adult children.

Elise receives a phone call from her brother-in-law to get the addresses of her married adult children. He wants to send them invitations to the upcoming temple marriage of his daughter. They talk for a while, and then Elise asks, "How's your family doing?"

He responds, "Pretty good, I guess, but we all feel bad that Jack (their sixteen-year-old son) didn't make the elite high school singing group that he really wanted to belong to. He worked hard for that, and we are all depressed that he's not going to be in it. How's your family?"

Elise says, "Okay." They say good-bye and she hangs up the phone and relates the conversation to her husband, Clark. She tells him about Jack not making the high school singing group, and that is the major concern of his family. They look at each other and start to laugh as they think about the seriousness of that problem in relation to what is happening to their own adult children. Their son-in-law Mark is out of work (again); their returned-missionary son Ralph is in love with a nonmember girl; their son Peter and his wife, Lori, have lost their testimonies and aren't going to church anymore; and they just found out that their daughter Helen has been convicted of auto theft and may be going to jail, leaving her two children without anyplace to go.

While Elise and Clark's family situation is no laughing matter, their ability to see humor is indicative of their healthy approach to their very serious problems. By choosing not to be completely weighed down by their oppressive challenges, they are not only increasing substantially the likelihood of their mental and emotional survival, but also their ability to deal meaningfully and effectively with their problem adult children. This is not an easy thing to do.

The tendency for many parents who are facing difficulties with their adult children is to allow themselves to be overcome. They have a number of things working against their peace of mind, including:

- Their perception that they have done something in the past to bring about their present predicaments, or that they are handling their situation poorly now.
- The trauma they are now facing.
- Their concern for what the future holds for their troubled children and for themselves.

This potential threefold burden is onerous for anyone to bear and can and should be relieved.

SELF-FLAGELLATION IS A FRUITLESS EXERCISE

You probably made some parenting mistakes while your children were growing up—everybody does. And you may even want to rethink what you are doing now with your adult children. After all, how many times have you gone through this parenting experience? It is OJT (on-the-job training) gained through trial and error. But since you are reading this book, it is obvious that you care about your adult children. That is a pretty good indication that you raised them the best way you knew how and that you want to do what is best for them now.

You need to put that realization in the bank and draw on it from time to time when you feel the urge to begin beating yourself. This is important because self-blame is often a major barrier that keeps parents from doing what is truly best for their children and an obstruction to the happiness of the parents.

The Lord does not require us to work beyond our abilities and externally established parameters (see Mosiah 4:27; D&C 10:4), and neither should we. We can only give what we have, and that is enough. To beat ourselves for something we cannot do, or for something we did or did not do, is a serious waste of valuable energy and is grossly counterproductive. Let the Lord fill in the gaps made by your inabilities, and be grateful that His grace is real—both for you and for your struggling adult children.

THE RESPONSIBILITY TO BE HAPPY

The Lord's plan for us has been designated a "plan of *happiness*" (see Alma 42:16). If we are not happy—*for the most part*—we better check what we are doing. We obviously are not letting the plan work *for* us. Whether or not we are happy needn't have much to do with what is happening to us externally. The promise is that if we are righteous and *seeking* to be happy, we will be (see Alma 27:18). So, we need to *choose* to be happy. As parents, that is our responsibility so that we can better bless our children. The following paragraphs list some of the reasons why we must choose to be happy and in control of our personal lives.

Children need to see the fruits of living the gospel. Ward and Estelle Roberts had been fretting for many months over the behavior of their oldest daughter, Becca, who was in her late teens. While they still allowed her to live with them (they felt they could best influence her if she was in their home), she was nearly impossible to live with. She was verbally abusive to them and to her younger siblings. She obeyed house rules only marginally (just enough to keep from being asked to leave), and Ward and Estelle suspected she was involved in immoral behavior and drug use.

They were consumed with Becca and her problems. Usually they were depressed, and they seldom laughed. Their involvement with their other children became perfunctory at best, as their thoughts were almost always centered on Becca. It was as though a dark cloud had settled upon their home and was overpowering everyone in it. Ward and Estelle had worked themselves into personal dysfunction, and it was affecting everyone else in the family.

Finally, they saw what was happening and talked about it. They could see that they were not allowing the light of the gospel to lift them or their children. They discussed how their personal examples should demonstrate the results of living the principles of the gospel so that Becca and the rest of their children could see firsthand that happiness came from following Jesus Christ. They vowed they would change and pleaded in their personal prayers for the strength to be happy.

They did change. It was not overnight and there were still periods of despondency, but by working to be happy, they began to see many things that they should be happy about. They also talked with their children about this, and all agreed to try to be better examples to Becca. Gradually the tension in the home subsided. While Becca did not noticeably change her behavior, the other children and Ward and Estelle became more comfortable around each other, and the joking and laughter that had been absent for so long began to return.

Becca ultimately went her own way and lived a life quite different from the other family members. Her lifestyle was not gospel centered, but she loved to come home because of the love and happiness that existed there. After a number of years, she began to go to Church again, and her nonmember husband asked to take the missionary lessons. He said he wanted to have in his home what he felt in Ward and Estelle's home.

How are adult children to know that the gospel of Jesus Christ brings happiness if their parents are not happy as they try to live it? How can they know that peace comes from righteousness, regardless of what one's external circumstances might be, if parents are not at peace in the midst of their own stresses? Parents who partake of the fruits the gospel offers doubly bless their children. The children see firsthand the blessings of living Christ's teachings so they can make choices accordingly, and they are being helped by parents who are *able* to help because of their own mental, emotional, and spiritual well-being.

Personal control brings peace, perspective, and increased capability. Adult children can cause parents great grief, but they do not have the power to take away their ability to function unless parents give it to them. Almost everything goes better for parents who are in control of their own lives. They think more clearly, have more energy, and are more resilient to traumatic "surprises" as well as chronic problems. They are better able to communicate and are less likely to create additional problems for themselves in other sectors of their lives. As a result of being in control, parents are much more likely to do and say those things which will meaningfully help a struggling adult child.

On the other hand, parents who cede their happiness and peace over to problem adult children effectively reduce, or even eliminate, their ability to help anyone. In fact, they become a problem themselves. In essence, personal peace is not so much a lofty ideal as it is a practical essential. Indeed, parental striving to achieve control over their own lives should, of necessity, be a top priority. Parents are not going to get very far until or unless they do this.

Homes need to be a place of peace. Mother and Dad are primarily responsible for the spirit that is in their homes. Ideally, homes should be:

- The most peaceful of all places for those who live there.
- Free of anger, unkind words, strife, or violence in any form.
- Places of protection and safety.
- Clean, comfortable, and orderly.
- The place where all members of the family would most like to be.

No home (or at least very few homes) meets this ideal completely. But parents who are trying to create such a home through their own example and effort will see progress. Over time, the peace and happiness that result will serve as a magnet to those adult children who are challenged and tend to draw them back to a lifestyle that will bring them that peace as well. The home will be a *good* place to be, and that, in and of itself, is enough reason to strive for this ideal.

WHAT CAN I DO TO BE HAPPIER?

Now comes the hard part. We have been talking about why it is important to be happy as we deal with our adult children, but how do you do it? Can you just say, "From now on I am going to be happy!" and you will be? Not quite—but almost. Happiness is a frame of mind, a perspective, a desire. To want to be happy is mandatory before one can ever be happy or at peace. There are quite a few things we can do to help us be happy:

Don't let problem adult children affect your happiness. Parents do not need to be dragged down emotionally, financially, spiritually, or physically by what their children do or do not do. Some troubled children expect their parents to be miserable like they are. That seems to be an eternal tendency (see 2 Ne. 2:18). Parents need to avoid that plunge into misery. They are entitled to the Lord's grace in doing so. The Lord has clearly taught that our own happiness or misery is contingent upon what we do, not what anyone else does (see, for example, Alma 3:26–27). If you want to be happy, then live the gospel. Remembering this truth can help parents stand strong when an adult child's whirlpool of woe threatens to suck them in.

Realize that time is on your side. Most challenges with adult children are not resolved quickly. This often brings a sense of frustration and futility to worried parents. In fact, time almost always works in favor of ultimate resolution. The important thing is to not let the unknown future gnaw on you to the point of chipping away your peace. We know a man who was confronted with a very serious problem with one of his adult children. The solution to the problem seemed to be completely out of his control. He lay awake fretting, then did an interesting piece of reasoning. He correctly concluded that there was nothing at all he could do about it right then. In the morning, he knew he would do what he could and that was all that would be expected of him. A few weeks from then, he knew this particular problem wouldn't be eating at him as much as it was now, and in a month, he would barely even be thinking about it. Since he wasn't going to be thinking much about it in the future, he reasoned, why worry about it now? He closed his eyes and went to sleep.

Granted, it isn't always that simple to talk ourselves out of a debilitating fret, but there is nothing wrong with our friend's logic. Try it. You will probably find it works.

Don't be concerned about what other people think. Most of us, whether we admit it or not, are very worried about what others think of us. This is particularly true of parents who are struggling with their adult children. After all, there, for everyone to see, is the evidence of what kind of parents we have been or are (or so it appears to parents who are having trouble with their children). Since such parents have likely been emotionally and spiritually battered and bruised already, they become extremely sensitive to further beatings their egos will take if they think that others are judging them harshly.

Let's not beat around the bush about this. There are many people who almost delight in seeing another family have serious problems.

Why? Because it makes their own problems seem less severe, or it makes them feel they haven't done so badly with their children if so-and-so is having that kind of problem with his children. Even some Church leaders are less than sympathetic to traumatized parents and tend to be judgmental because they have not yet had such experiences with their own children.

So how do parents who are facing difficult challenges handle this perceived or actual harsh judgment from friends or leaders? We could say just slough it off, ignore it, close your eyes to it. But this is probably nearly impossible to do, especially in the beginning of such trials. What is more doable is to hit the challenge head-on. Deal with it, then get on with life. To do this successfully, strive to:

- Not judge the person who you think is judging you.
- Realize that only you and your Heavenly Father know the circumstances here and are the only ones, therefore, who are qualified to make any kind of judgment.
- Seek Heavenly Father's help; He understands.

Overcoming the tendency to be affected by what others may think of you as a parent is never easy. Over time, it gets easier. It is important that parents who want to be happy learn to do this.

Take a break from your challenges. Some parents are so distressed by their difficult adult children that they stop doing the very things that will bring them a semblance of peace and balance in their lives. Hobbies are forgotten, exercising stops, recreational activities are foregone, and vacations are not taken. This is a mistake. Parents need to keep doing the things that have brought them relaxation and enjoyment in the past. These activities are more than pleasure; they are therapeutic. They are necessary pauses that allow parents to regroup emotionally and renew spiritually. If you haven't developed a hobby before, get one now. Keep up with your weekly spouse dates, or start them if you haven't been doing them. If you have been putting off a vacation until things get better, go on it now so things *can* get better.

Lose yourself in service. When we are helping others, we need less help ourselves. In some profound way, the act of service relieves the burdens of those who are serving. We have watched bishops and stake presidents, Relief Society and Primary teachers, Young Men and Young Women advisers, and home teachers and visiting teachers have their extraordinary emotional and spiritual burdens associated with their errant adult children lifted as a result of their dedicated and compassionate service in the Church. Service is a balm.

There is one caution here, however. Some parents would use service to others as an excuse for not dealing with their own adult child's severe problems. While we should not stop our assistance to others, we should never rationalize away our responsibility to help our own children because of the service we are rendering to someone or something outside our family.

Take time to "be still." It is usually only in spiritual solitude that we are able to hear the quiet whisperings of God (see Ps. 46:10). Ultimately, peace comes through the Spirit dwelling within us. That Spirit does not exist amidst mental and emotional noise and confusion. Or, at least, we will not understand it or feel it (see 3 Ne. 11:3–6). Of necessity, we must remove ourselves, from time to time, from the loud distractions of the world and from our spiritually deafening problems if we are ever to be happy. Appropriate stillness can be obtained through pondering the scriptures, quiet walks, partaking of the sacrament, attending the temple, and offering up our oblation of a broken heart and contrite spirit through prayer in our closets and silent places. Taking the time to "be still" will bring us the stillness of the Spirit we call peace.

Finding peace and happiness amidst trials and challenges is possible. It is a decision we must make. We must strive to "press forward with a steadfastness in Christ, having a perfect brightness of hope" (see 2 Ne. 31:20). If we want it, we will then do what is necessary to obtain it. And that we can do.

HAVING HOPE

Surely there is nothing that has greater influence on the present peace of parents than their hope (or lack of it) that the problems with their adult children will be resolved sometime in the future. Indeed, that hope says everything about whether parents will continue to devote time and resources to those children. If there is no hope that parental sacrifice is ultimately going to have positive results, why try? If there is no hope that errant adult children will ever change—either here in this telestial tour or sometime in the eternities—can there ever be peace for those who have nurtured them, loved them, and sacrificed for them?

Are parents justified in hoping that regardless of how impossible change in a troubled child may seem now, such change will sometime, somewhere come about? We think so. We are promised in sacred places that we will have rejoicing in our children. That time may be slow in coming. The wait may be long and frustrating. But it is a promise from the Lord and is based upon the *faithfulness of the parents*. We have control of our faithfulness, and that ought to give us hope in the ultimate positive outcome of our efforts on behalf of our children. The Apostle Paul taught that "whatsoever things were written aforetime were written for our learning, that we through patience and comfort of the scriptures might have hope" (Rom. 15:4).

With Paul's encouragement in mind, the words of Boyd K. Packer, Acting President of the Quorum of the Twelve, should bring us some hope. He said, "The measure of our success as parents . . . will not rest solely on how our children turn out [in this life]. . . . It is not uncommon for responsible parents to lose one of their children, for a time, to influences over which they have no control." He continued, quoting Elder Orson F. Whitney of the Quorum of the Twelve Apostles: "'Though some of the sheep may wander, the eye of the Shepherd is upon them, and sooner or later they will feel the tentacles of Divine Providence reaching out after them and drawing them back to the fold. . . . Hope on, trust on, till you see the salvation of God'" ("Our Moral Environment," *Ensign*, May 1992, 68).

President Gordon B. Hinckley, when he was First Counselor in the First Presidency, said to those who were striving to raise their children in the light of the gospel: "I make you a solemn and sacred promise that if you will do this, the time will come when, looking upon those you have created, nurtured, and loved, you will see the fruits of your nurturing and get on your knees and thank the Lord for His blessing to you" ("Bring Up a Child in the Way He Should Go," *Ensign*, November 1993, 60).

We ought to find "patience and comfort," as Paul admonished us to do, in these words of latter-day prophets. Parents must know that their efforts are well worth the price, and that can only be understood by seeing parenthood in its true eternal perspective. This knowledge does not proclaim freedom from worrying about or raising and associating with adult children who have strayed, or are otherwise troublesome, but brings cause for hope and peace and happiness—even in the middle of great stress.

PONDERING THE PRINCIPLE

Our own happiness has much to do with our ability to bless our adult children. It has everything to do with our capacity to hold on when the actions of our grown-up children are bringing us grief. Happiness is an attitude, a perception of life. As such, we have a great deal of control over it. While outside forces can bring discouragement, even a sense of futility at times, we have ultimate command over our own state of mind. Happiness, in essence, is a choice.

- Parental obsession with self-blame for real or imagined shortcomings is counterproductive.
- Parents have a responsibility to be happy.
- Homes that are places of peace tend to draw errant adult children back to those values that once made them happy.
- Parents should not let their ultimate happiness be affected by the actions of their adult children.
- Time usually works in favor of parents who are struggling with errant children.
- Negative remarks or thoughts from others can be overcome by parents who will not respond in kind and who seek the Lord for strength.
- Parents who continue to involve themselves in healthy recreational activities and hobbies are better able to handle difficulties with their adult children.
- Parents who lose themselves in serving others find their own burdens are lifted as well.

- The Lord has promised that righteous parents will have joy in their posterity, which should give reason for ultimate hope to all such parents.

Peace and happiness come through living the principles of the gospel of Jesus Christ, but it isn't always easy to keep that peace and happiness from being overshadowed by the pain and sorrow that is inevitable when our adult children stray. Through the grace of Christ, though, it can be done—if that is our desire. God's plan for us is a plan of happiness. We need to let it work that way in our lives.

QUESTIONS & ANSWERS

Q I have been so devastated with what is happening with my twenty-six-year-old daughter that I can't seem to get a grip on my own life. She is doing graduate work at a major university and is living with a self-proclaimed atheist. Now she has renounced the Church and its teachings as a bunch of myths and unenlightened rules. She attended seminary all four years, graduated from BYU, and then did a 180-degree turn. I can't get this out of my mind. I can't eat and I can't sleep. I know I'm not going to help my daughter until I get control of myself, but I don't seem to be able to do that. What can I do?

A Your greatest source of strength is going to be the Savior. His Atonement was to relieve burdens, which includes this one of yours. Ask God for help. That strength will come over time. In the meantime, you need to be doing what you can to focus on those things that will bring you some peace. We have outlined some of these in this chapter. Try them.

Q If you don't have a husband and are dealing with adult children who are messing up their lives, it isn't easy to keep a strong and positive outlook when you are having to do this all alone. How do you keep a positive attitude then?

A You do it the same way you would if you had a husband. While you don't have someone next to you to commiserate with, you can still choose to be happy. You have to work at this whether you are

married or not. In fact, sometimes it can even be harder to be positive when you are married, especially when your spouse becomes
part of the problem because of his or her negative attitude. Don't
let your situation stand in the way of striving to be happy. Just do
the best you can and you will be okay.

Q Say all you want about parents not taking the blame for their
adult children's wrong behavior, but I *am* to blame. I'm a worka-
holic and was hardly ever with my children when they were
growing up. I just didn't want to be bothered with anything other
than my work. Now none of my children is active in the Church,
and they don't really want much to do with me either. I've
changed, but I've made a mess of my children's lives. I don't know
what to do now. Any suggestions?

A We didn't say parents should never take the blame. We said that
parents should not let their concern for what they did (whether it
actually had a negative effect on their children or not) keep them
from doing now what they ought to do. If you feel you have done
wrong by your children in the past, go to them and apologize. Tell
them you want to be a better father now and ask them for the
chance to be so. Then be better. You initiate contact with them,
love them, and show them by your own life the peace and happiness that comes from being an active, committed member of the
Church. Be patient—with them and with yourself.

Q My oldest son just recently died of AIDS. How can you just turn
that off and get on with your life?

A You can't just turn it off, but you can learn to live with it. The
important thing is to not dissociate yourself emotionally from
your other children and your husband as you are striving to deal
with this. They are at least as important a part of your family as is
your deceased son, and you need to try to remember that. You
need to be happy for their sakes, as well as for your own.

Q We have three children—eighteen, nineteen, and twenty-two—who
still live with us, but they fight a lot among themselves. Every time
I mention it, the situation gets worse. What should I do?

A Call a family council and discuss your concerns. Let them help you come up with some ideas that could be used to bring some peace into your home. Get commitments from them to try to do better. If there is not progress, you may want to insist that the contention stop. It is your home, after all, and they are there as guests at your invitation. You have a right to have a peaceful home, and they have the responsibility to abide by the rules of the house. If they still refuse, you have the option to ask them to leave.

Q When do parents become smart again? My children often tell me how dumb I am, and it hurts. I keep waiting for them to grow up and appreciate me as I am.

A This is rude and inexcusable. Your adult children need to act like adults, and this is unacceptable. Sit them down and tell them how much their words hurt and ask them to be kinder and more patient with you. If they still continue to do this, you may want to limit your involvement with them until they do some changing. This is their problem, not yours.

Q Whenever I sit in a sacrament meeting and the speaker talks about all of his children being married in the temple, I feel lousy. Only two of our children married in the temple, and two married nonmembers. I vacillate between feeling that we have not been very good parents and thinking that the speaker thinks too much of himself just because he was lucky that all of his children "stuck." I don't want to feel this way, but I do. How can I stop feeling like this?

A Just try to remember that every family is unique. Every child is different, and every parent is distinct. In addition, the economic, spiritual, and social environment that each family exists in is not the same. You cannot legitimately make comparisons between one family and another or between one set of parents and another. If you are doing the best you can do, that is what is important, and that should bring you some peace. One thing that is bound to destroy that potential peace is making judgments about someone else. Don't do it. You'll enjoy your sacrament meetings a lot more.

Q My wife and I have talked about going on a mission now that our children are all grown, but we are reluctant to go because we feel our oldest daughter, who is divorced and raising three children, needs us nearby for support. She says we ought to go, but we babysit the children often, and I help fix things around her house and make sure her car is running. What do you think we should do?

A If your daughter feels she is okay without you, you should go. It will be a great blessing to you, and you will be setting an important example of Church service for your daughter and her children. In fact, it will probably be good for them to not have you so close by for a while so that they can develop some needed independence. You should keep in close contact with them by letter and by phone while you are away.

Q I have brothers and sisters who were what I consider to be unrighteous and aggravating throughout their lives, even up to their deaths. They never changed. Why should I think that my errant adult children will change? Didn't Heavenly Father lose one-third of all of His children?

A The Church teaches that none of the children that Heavenly Father lost will be born on this earth. All who made it here or will make it here, including your siblings and your children, were valiant before they came. They were neither fence-sitters nor rebellious, but faithful to God and to the Savior. Why should we automatically think that "problem" adult children have "permanently" changed from who they were? We don't know, for example, what role chemical imbalances, emotional and mental deficiencies, environmental conditions, and just plain lack of knowledge play in our decision making here. We do know they are factors. It seems to us that we ought to follow the example of the prophets in giving our children (and our siblings) the eternal benefit of the doubt and act accordingly. In other words, don't ever give up hope!

CHAPTER 9

SAY IT, AND SAY IT RIGHT

Principle 9: Parents who seek to communicate frequently, accurately, and lovingly with their adult children are likely to see relationships improve and their children behave more responsibly.

Darrel and Megan Snow were preparing to move out of state. Jennifer, their nineteen-year-old daughter, confronted them as they were ready to leave. "I am not going to move with you. I haven't been living the gospel very well, and I'm not very happy with myself. You won't be very happy with me either. You go live your lives and forget about me. I will live mine." Talk about a bombshell!

Darrel and Megan were numb, but they decided to make the move without their daughter. They really had little choice, but after the move they wondered if they had done the right thing. Jennifer, in the meantime, found herself living several states away from her parents and was facing problems far more difficult to deal with than she had ever imagined. Life was very hard for her, and she felt alone. She knew her parents were worried, but she still didn't want to face them.

Darrel and Megan continued to worry about what their role in Jennifer's life should be. They respected her right to stay behind and deal with her own problems, but they also wanted her to know that they were willing to help her if she wanted it. They had maintained telephone communication with Jennifer all along, but after praying and fasting, the Snows decided to take another step with her. Darrel called his daughter and asked if she would meet with him. She was hesitant, but agreed, and he made arrangements to see her.

On the appointed day, Darrel flew to the city they had moved from, and Jennifer picked him up at the airport. After some time, she finally agreed to drive to a place where they could talk in private. The discussion didn't start out that well. Jennifer expressed some bitterness and resentment as she talked about her reasons for not wanting to be around her parents anymore. Darrel patiently told her that his purpose for wanting to meet with her was to see if he could help her resolve some of her problems and to offer their resources if needed. During the long talk, they both shed tears. After that, they were able to work out a satisfactory solution.

Darrel and Megan's desire to communicate with Jennifer and make clear to her their concern and willingness to assist her in meaningful ways had a powerful impact. The meeting proved to be a literal turning point in Jennifer's life. She has since married in the temple and moved closer to her parents. Not too long ago, she called Darrel and Megan and invited them to lunch. With considerable emotion, she thanked her parents for saving her life.

Would Jennifer have turned herself around if her parents had not decided to make that extraordinary effort to communicate with her? Maybe so, but probably not when she did. Darrel and Megan were certain they did the right thing and were grateful that their patient efforts brought forth fruit. Even if Jennifer had not responded as she did, they knew that they had at least done everything they could do.

For many parents, one of the hardest things they face is knowing how and when to communicate with their adult children. This is particularly challenging when a pattern of consistent, healthy communication was not established as the child was growing up. Sometimes parents are bashful and reserved. They don't feel comfortable getting into sustained conversations with anyone, particularly when there is a chance that it might be unpleasant.

More often than not, however, parent–adult child communication suffers because one or more of the parties feel that open communication will damage their relationship. This is particularly the case when present relationships are fragile anyway or if any of the participants have had challenges with temper in past exchanges. In some instances, parents feel that previous attempts to communicate have failed and have been hurtful. They are fearful of trying again.

Regardless of the reasons why parents limit their communication with their adult children, those who will consistently strive to overcome that reticence and seek to improve and increase their dialogue will generally find that their children will *eventually* respond positively to that effort. Over time, chances are that relationships will improve and more responsible behavior will result.

GOOD COMMUNICATION IS IMPORTANT

Peter and Roxanne felt deep concern for their daughter Jan, who seemed to be going nowhere. They met with her and openly discussed their expectations and hopes as well as their concerns. Jan responded immediately by agreeing to go to school. She simply had not known that her education mattered to them, and she was glad to have some direction in her life. Compliance dates and financing were discussed, and each person's responsibilities were identified and agreed upon. The meeting cleared the air, opening the way for the family to work together for Jan's benefit.

Jan's parents took one of the first steps in communicating: they talked. Simple, isn't it? But parents often assume their children know what their parents think, expect, or require of them and that they, the parents, know what their adult children think and expect from them, even though nothing has been directly said about it. Many of the challenges occurring between parents and adult children stem from this likely erroneous assumption and the consequent lack of communication. In fact, communication is the basic tool through which almost every family problem can be resolved or prevented, *if it can be resolved or prevented at all.*

Good communication helps prevent misunderstandings, provides needed information so that better decisions can be made, and can establish an atmosphere of cooperation and conciliation that is necessary for parent–adult child relationships to be the best they can be.

WAYS TO COMMUNICATE

There are many ways for parents to maintain communication with their adult children. If used effectively, the ways listed here can bless your relationship.

Letter writing. Generally more formal than informal. This has been around since the beginning of time, but is one of the most difficult communication devices to use. For one thing, it takes more time than most other ways to communicate the same amount of information. Since that is the case, letters tend to be more focused than other forms of communication. In addition, because a letter can be held onto and read and reread, more care is usually taken (or should be taken) in its composition than in other types of communication. Because a good letter takes so much effort to write (particularly one that is handwritten), the recipient of the letter knows the writer is interested in him or her and desires to communicate something that is important.

E-mail. Generally informal. This modern form of letter writing is quick, easy, and cheap to use. It allows the sender to distribute the same message to a number of people, thus increasing the efficiency of communication. However, because it is so fast and simple, it may not show the same degree of personal interest as a letter.

Telephone. Generally informal. Although this is perhaps the most expensive, it is also the preferred communication device for most parents and their adult children. It not only allows for the communication of thoughts and ideas, but feelings can be manifest as well through the tone and volume of the voices. The ability of those listening to respond immediately to what the other person has just said makes the communication that much more complete and effective.

Personal conversations. Very informal. Because these communications usually occur on the spur of the moment and as a natural part of social living, they are generally the least threatening of all communications. Consequently, what is said in these discussions is less likely to be taken as seriously, and, therefore, be as impacting, as what is communicated in other ways. That is not to say, however, that serious points cannot be made in the course of an informal conversation. In fact, because of the casual nature of the conversation, an adult child may be more receptive to a well-thought-out statement by the parent than if the same statement were made in a more formal setting. On the other hand, serious damage to relationships can occur in such casual conversations when potentially hurtful things are said, even in a "playful" way. Regardless of how innocuous a conversation may be, the wrong word or tone can be devastating to a parent–adult child relationship, especially if that relationship is fragile to begin with.

Family councils. Generally formal. When there are specific family problems that need to be dealt with, a family council can be called to discuss what those problems are and to assign responsibilities. A form of family council, the Responsibility Meeting, will be discussed in detail in this chapter. These meetings are focused, usually follow an agenda, and are intended to arrive at solutions.

Most parents use most, if not all, of these ways to communicate with their adult children. Which communication avenues are used depends on the technical skills of the parents and children, their geographic proximity to one another, their comfort or convenience with one way or another, and their budget limitations. Furthermore, as a general rule, *the more serious (or potentially serious) the topic or intent, the more formal the means of communication should be.* The corollary to this rule, of course, is that the less serious the concern, the less formal the communication. For example, parents are probably not going to call a Responsibility Meeting when their returned-missionary son who is living with them comes in one morning at 3:00 A.M. They would likely have a casual conversation about it. However, if the pattern continued, a Responsibility Meeting would likely be of benefit.

There lies with all parents the responsibility to strive for regular communication with their adult children, using those means which they feel most comfortable with and can afford and which correspond to the message they wish to convey.

EFFECTIVE COMMUNICATION

Few parents are experts in communication, and virtually all of us wish we could take back some things we have said or change how we said it. That's part of learning how to be a parent. What we have found to be most important in communicating is the desire or intent of the parent. If that desire is centered on the well-being of the child, and therefore based on love, that intent will usually be felt by the child regardless of how awkward the communication attempt is. Parents should never be so caught up with improving their communication technique that they let an emphasis on technique detract from their desire to help the child.

This does not mean, however, that parents do not need to evaluate their communication knowledge and skills. They should do this continually, then strive to make the appropriate adjustments. How and when you say something will often affect the message that is conveyed. Conscientious parents will earnestly try to make their communication what they want it to be.

The pattern the Savior gave to His priesthood holders in dealing with others provides meaningful direction to all parents. The Savior has instructed that our communications are to be based on the principles of "persuasion" rather than force, "long-suffering" rather than reactiveness, "gentleness" as opposed to harshness, and "meekness" rather than arrogance or loftiness, and on love that is true and sincere. Parents' speech should be kind rather than cruel and should be based on "pure knowledge" rather than innuendo, rumor, or unfounded assumption (see D&C 121:41–42). When parents give counsel, they need to be trying to live it themselves; otherwise, hypocrisy will undermine anything that they say. Parents should avoid being clever or tricky in their delivery, but rather try to be straightforward, clear, and honest. Sometimes it may be necessary to reprimand "with sharpness," but this is to be done at the appropriate moment and when the Spirit whispers that it will help. Afterwards, parents should strive to "[show] forth . . . an increase of love" to the adult child so that he or she may know that what was said was for that child's good (see D&C 121:43–44). Easier said than done, huh?

Here are some other communication tips that will be helpful:

- Parents should try to do what they say they will do, or future communication may be undermined.
- When parents have made *reasonable* efforts to communicate with a challenged adult child and that child has not responded, decisions that normally would have been discussed between the parents and the child may need to be made unilaterally by the parents.
- Parents should strive to listen to what their adult child

is saying. They may need to ask questions and repeat back until they are reasonably certain they understand.

- Parents ought to be unambiguous and thorough in communicating their expectations, assignments, or consequences for noncompliance. Too much detail is generally better than too little.
- Parents should be responsive to reasonable counsel from their adult children.
- Parents should try to end all communication sessions positively with some expression of love, gratitude, or praise for the child.
- Parents should readily apologize when they feel that what they have said to their adult child or the way they have said it was inappropriate.
- Parents who are striving to do their best in communicating can know they are doing enough.

When communicating with married children, parents should:

- Contact them regularly by phone or mail. Try to talk to both the husband and wife if they call.
- Try to visit them face-to-face as often as possible. Visit with *both* the husband and wife when they are with them.
- Speak to them as equals.
- Not gossip about other family members.
- Include both the husband and wife if they feel they need to hold a Responsibility Meeting.

No one communicates perfectly, and not every problem is solved even when there is good communication. *Trying* to keep the lines of communication open and *trying* to communicate effectively is a manifestation of parental love that will tend to soften the heart of a challenged adult child. It will also go a long way toward preventing potential problems from ever arising.

THE RESPONSIBILITY MEETING

When troubles arise that may involve parents' time, money, home, or other resources that are being shared with their adult children, it is often helpful for parents to plan a meeting with their children to identify the *expectations* and *responsibilities* of all parties. We call this a Responsibility Meeting. It is essentially a family council that is limited to those directly involved in a concern. It should be a meeting of understanding and discussion and often serves to clear the air, creating feelings of harmony.

In a Responsibility Meeting, participants expect to evaluate each problem on the agenda and to agree upon a plan for resolution. The goal is to teach and encourage mature, responsible behavior among family members by establishing clear parameters with respect to parental resources and explicit behavioral expectations on the part of all who are involved.

In this light, it is important to understand that this is *not* a democratic meeting. While compromise and conciliation should be sought after, those (usually the parents) who bring the most to the table make the ultimate decision in case of disagreement. This is their meeting, and it is under their control. The desired outcome should always be peace that comes from a spirit of understanding, cooperation, and agreement. But that doesn't always happen. It is possible for a Responsibility Meeting to be "successful," even when the parties do not agree. If communication has taken place, expectations are understood, and consequences have been clearly explained, the Responsibility Meeting has accomplished much. Depending on the attitude and maturity of the adult child, this may bring a temporary "war" rather than an immediate peace. But that communication will ultimately work in everyone's best interests if the parents' motives are what they should be.

Here are some ideas to make Responsibility Meetings more likely to succeed.

Deciding if and when to hold a Responsibility Meeting. The purpose of the Responsibility Meeting is to clarify and communicate understanding between parents and adult children regarding parent resources that are either currently being shared with the adult children or are anticipated to be shared. A Responsibility Meeting should therefore be held when there is actual, perceived, or anticipated misunderstanding or dissatisfaction on the part of either the parents or the adult children with respect to the sharing of those resources. While sometimes an adult child may initiate such a meeting, it is almost always the parents' call whether such a meeting is held. It is the parents' resource that is being shared, and it will generally be their anxiety about their unfulfilled behavioral expectations of their adult children, or the children's challenges with perceived unreasonable parental expectations, that is the catalyst for this meeting to be held. If the decision is made to hold a Responsibility Meeting, it should be held as soon as is reasonably possible. To put it off is likely to deepen and widen the gap of dissatisfaction and misunderstanding that the meeting is being called to bridge. Obviously, it is almost always better to hold such a meeting *before* resources are shared, rather than after.

Who should attend the meeting? Generally, only parents and the adult child (with spouse if he or she is married) or adult children who are specifically involved should be at this meeting. Bringing others into the discussion sometimes creates distractions and can dilute the potential effectiveness of the meeting. An exception would be a single mother who might need some outside-the-family support. It is usually unnecessary (and undesirable) to ever have a third-party mediator.

What to do before the meeting. Parents should plan the meeting *before* they announce it. They should decide between themselves the following three things:

- What they would like to have happen: for example, what the "perfect" solution would be. They should strive for this objective.
- What they could live with: solutions that are less than they would like, but acceptable under the circumstances. An example might be a timed phase-out of a disagreeable adult child action, rather than it being stopped immediately.
- What they cannot live with: solutions that are completely unacceptable to them. No matter what happens,

this outcome will not be allowed. An example might be an adult child wanting to keep stolen things.

Parents should try to be very specific and agree as to what will be on the agenda and what will and will not be acceptable outcomes. A written agenda should be prepared, with the specific items that are to be the subject of the meeting. This list is *not* published, nor is it discussed beforehand with the adult child. The meeting should then be announced, well in advance, and a copy of the agenda given to the adult child. Parents communicate to the adult child that these problems need to be resolved at this meeting. Parents should go to the meeting in the right spirit, praying and even fasting if appropriate, and they should invite their adult child to do the same.

How to get your adult child to the table. Getting cooperative adult children to the Responsibility Meeting is usually not a problem. Just explain to them what you want to talk about (show them the agenda), coordinate the meeting time, and ask them to be there. Troubled adult children can pose a challenge. They have a natural reluctance to be involved in any kind of situation that is going to be uncomfortable for them or require of them more than they are currently doing. Parents ought to proceed with trying to get them to the Responsibility Meeting anyway. The steps to take, in this order, would be to:

- Ask them kindly, but firmly, to be in attendance. Make every effort to make the time and place for the meeting convenient and pleasant for them. If they refuse to come, then:
- Indicate your awareness of how difficult this is for them, but affirm that it is important for this discussion to take place. If they still refuse, then:
- State that unless they agree to attend a Responsibility Meeting, no action will be taken regarding any of their requests to share your resources with them or that you will determine unilaterally what you will or will not do and what your expectations of them will be in order for you to be willing to share any resources. If they still refuse, then:

- Remain true to your word. Make your decisions without their input. Write those decisions out and give a copy to ☆ them so there will be no misunderstanding about what you have decided.

Where to hold the Responsibility Meeting. There are two factors that will determine where the meeting is to be held: how formal you want the meeting to be and what is feasible. Responsibility Meetings can be held just about anywhere—on the phone, in the car, at home, or in some other place. The general rule is the more serious the problem, the more formal the communication setting. The best place for a Responsibility Meeting is usually in the home of the parents, which is generally a more formal setting than others. Perhaps the least desirable place to hold this meeting (and the least formal) is over the telephone, because you do not have eye contact, you cannot read body language, and it is easier for the adult child to leave it (he just needs to hang up). While the location of a Responsibility Meeting is important, that it is held is even more critical. Find the best location you can, and hold the meeting.

How to effectively conduct a Responsibility Meeting. Regardless of where the Responsibility Meeting is held, there is a pattern that can be followed to make it as effective as possible.

- Either the father or the mother conducts—usually the father.
- Seek the Spirit.
- Open and close with prayer.
- Avoid speaking angrily or condescendingly.
- State clearly the objective of the meeting.
- Have a written agenda and stay focused on it.
- Seek open discussion concerning challenging areas, and listen carefully to what the adult child says.
- Seek acceptable compromises regarding resource sharing, responsibilities of the adult child, and consequences of unacceptable actions.
- Make specific decisions, even if there is not child agreement. These decisions need to include details concerning what resources are to be shared with the

adult child, what is required of the adult child, and
when it is required.

- State clearly the decisions reached, make certain they are
  understood, and write them out for future reference.
- Schedule follow-up sessions to monitor progress or to
  modify decisions.
- Express your love.
- Do what you say you will do.
- Follow up systematically according to the specified
  timetable.

A Responsibility Meeting planned and conducted in a spirit of
love and kindness is one of the most effective communication tools
available to help solve and prevent problems with adult children.
While it will never fix everything and sometimes does not accomplish
what we expect it to, it almost always clears the air and takes us a step
closer to an acceptable resolution of our children's challenges.

MEASURING THE SUCCESS OF OUR COMMUNICATION ATTEMPTS

For some parents, only a complete resolution of an existing
problem, or the elimination of a potential problem, demonstrates that
their communication efforts with their adult children have been effective. We need to be more realistic than this. For one thing, it does not
often happen. Some problems with adult children will never be
resolved in this lifetime, no matter how hard parents try or how well
they communicate. Usually, we measure our success "here a little and
there a little." Parents can be reasonably certain that their communication is being effective:

- If there is any noticeable positive change in the behavior
  of the adult child.
- If overall understanding has increased and parent–
  adult child relationships are improved as a result.
- If adult children clearly understand the consequences
  of their actions and parental expectations for them so

they can exercise their agency with full knowledge of the potential results.

Once again, it is only necessary that parents do what they can do. The rest will take care of itself.

SOME REALLY DUMB THINGS PARENTS SAY TO THEIR ADULT CHILDREN

One of the most frustrating things for parents of adult children is when they say something that to them is completely innocuous but ends up being offensive to their children. Worse still is when parents don't even know they have just widened the trust gap between them and their children because of what they just said. Most of the time, these statements offend the adult child because they are condescending in their assumption, if not in their tone. Some of them may have been okay to say when the child was a "kid," but now they potentially hurt. And some of them were never okay to say.

Here are a few of those really dumb things parents are tempted to say. Our advice? Resist the temptation!

To Your Single Adult Child:
Where is my change?
Are you still saying your prayers every day?
Adults don't behave like that.
When (older brother or sister) was your age, he or she was . . .
Do you realize how much we give to you?
You need a haircut.
Did you bathe this morning?
If you're not making A's, you're wasting my money.
When was the last time you went to church?
I don't want to hear your excuses.
How come you're not wearing a tie to church?
Where do you spend all of your money?
Why did you do that?
Why are you wearing that outfit?
You can't afford to buy that car! (after the car is bought)

Why don't you comb your hair?
That was a stupid thing to do.
You marry whom you date.
I don't know where you picked up that nasty habit.
You ought to date more.
Why weren't you more careful with my car?
What happened to that boy who asked you out last week?
If you'd listen to me, you'd be a lot better off.
When are you ever going to get married?
Stop eating so much junk food.
If you'd lose a little weight, you'd get more dates.
I don't think she's your type.
If you really cared about us, you wouldn't do that.

To Your Married Adult Child:
Don't get pregnant until you have both finished school.
Are you pregnant again?
Don't name your baby that!
You're married; you need to be more responsible.
What are you doing that is making your husband so unhappy?
When are you going to have another baby?
Why don't you just teach your kids to clean their rooms?
I thought I taught you how to cook better than that!
Are your kids eating okay? They don't look healthy.
When are you going to give us our dresser back?
How long has it been since you changed this baby?
You want to borrow how much?
Your drapes and sofa don't match.
We were never in debt except for a home.
How much did you pay for that boat?
Can't you stop your kids from running around the house?
Do you want me to cut his hair?
How can you afford to go on a trip like that?
I hope you don't think I'm interfering, but . . .
If he were my kid, I'd spank him!
How come you're not a high priest yet?
Do you go to the temple every month?

People will think you were raised in a dirty house.

I told you not to marry him.

We aren't going to be able to babysit. We're not as young as we used to be, you know.

When you get to be our age . . .

You kids never fought like that when you were your children's ages.

And on and on. You get the idea. Just be careful. A good rule of thumb is to talk to your adult child as you would any other adult—as a peer, not as an inexperienced adolescent. That may require a change in the way you see your adult child. You will be wise to make that change as quickly and as completely as you can—for your adult child's sake, and for your own.

PONDERING THE PRINCIPLE

No relationships between parents and their adult children will ever be as good as they can be until parents have done all they can to establish meaningful communication with their children. While parents who put forth the effort to communicate frequently and effectively are not assured their adult children will respond in a positive way anytime soon, chances are they ultimately will. At the very least, such parents have opened doors to that possibility. In the case of intransigent children, such parental communication attempts seem to be unilateral and ineffective, but at least there is communication, and the child is aware of the parents' position and love. This is significant and positive.

- Parents who are naturally reserved need to strive to overcome their shyness by being proactive in establishing consistent, effective communication with their children.
- If parents don't say it, their adult children may not know it.
- Good family communication is the means by which most parent–adult child problems are resolved—if they can be resolved.
- Wise parents use the form of communication that will

most likely exemplify the tone of what they wish to communicate. Generally, the more serious the subject, the more formal the communication.

- Parental intent is always more important than parental communication skills.
- Parents should be willing to honestly evaluate their communication skills and try to make the appropriate adjustments.
- Responsibility Meetings are effective tools in establishing expectations and consequences with respect to the use of parental resources by adult children.
- Parents need to be patient in evaluating the results of their communication attempts with their adult children. Successes often come in small increments and frequently only after significant time.

It is not necessary that parents be perfect in their communication skills. It is important that they are doing the best they can and that they are consistent in those efforts. Some communication will inevitably take place, no matter how fragile the relationships. Parents who are prayerfully and lovingly striving to improve those relationships through their communication will likely see progress. They will certainly have the peace that comes from knowing they are doing all they can.

QUESTIONS & ANSWERS

Q I never felt very comfortable talking with my children about their responsibilities while they were growing up. It always seemed to open the door to complaints and disagreeable conversations, and I don't like that, so I didn't often get into those kinds of discussions with them. Should I try to change that now?

A Absolutely, if you want your relationship with them to improve. Probably the reason they were complaining and disagreeable in such conversations is that they knew you would stop the conversation and leave them alone—without their having to change their misbehavior that brought on the conversation in the first place. Rather than stopping the contention, your reluctance to call your children on the carpet probably added to it. You need to let your children know you will hold them accountable for unacceptable behavior. Then do it. They will see that their complaining and unpleasant responses don't get them off the hook, and they will likely modify their reaction accordingly. Be patient with them, but be consistent.

Live at home? Live our core values/standards.

Q What do you do when an adult child refuses to accept parental counsel?

A It depends on whether or not you are sharing any of your resources with him. If he is living with you or you are assisting him in any way, you might consider basing your assistance on his heeding your counsel. You need to communicate your expectations, and such a tie-in, clearly and kindly. He can then make his choice as to what he wants to do—abide by your counsel and continue to receive your help, or not follow your counsel and forfeit that help. If you are not presently assisting him, all you can do is give him counsel and hope he follows it. If he doesn't, maybe you should stop giving it. Continue to love him, though, and keep attempting to communicate.

Q We have never had good communication with our errant daughter. How do we start now?

A In order for "good" communication to take place, it has to be two-way. Other than striving to keep communication channels open and treating your daughter with respect and kindness, there is not much else you can do if she doesn't want to participate in any kind of meaningful dialogue. However, there can still be "acceptable" communication. If you are sharing your resources with her, you can ask her to come to the table to discuss what will be required of her to continue receiving those resources. If she is dependent on those resources, it is probable that she will meet with you. You can use such communication opportunities to express love and to give counsel. Since you are the provider, you have the right to specify your expectations of her and spell out consequences that will result if those expectations are not met.

Regardless of her attitude, such meetings allow you to communicate to her clearly what you want her to know and, over time, can lead to communication opportunities that are satisfying to both parties.

Q My daughter and her husband (and their new baby) moved into my basement with the promise to help with the meals and the yard if they could live rent-free while going to school. It worked well for a month or two, but now, two years later, they do nothing. From time to time I have mentioned our agreement to them, and they say they will do it, but don't. Our relationship is going downhill fast. What should I do?

A A casual conversation with your daughter and son-in-law about the situation is obviously not going to change anything. If you continue like you are, your relationship may be so damaged that it will take years to heal. You need to hold a Responsibility Meeting with them. Decide beforehand what you want the outcome of that meeting to be ideally (e.g., they will do consistently what they originally agreed to do) and what some acceptable less-than-perfect alternatives might be (e.g., they will pay you rent for the days or weeks they do not help). You should also know what consequences you are willing to apply if they do not perform acceptably (e.g., move out of your basement). Then call your meeting. Have a prayer, outline your concerns, have a discussion, and then state what you have decided will happen. If they do not agree to what you want done, then be willing to carry through with your predetermined consequences. If they say they will do what you ask, set a time for a future Responsibility Meeting to review their performance and make appropriate modifications. Stick to your guns, and follow through.

Q I just can't see how I would ever sit down with my adult children and hold a meeting with them. I don't like formal meetings, and they don't like them either. Can't I accomplish the same thing talking to them over the phone or in a regular conversation?

A Maybe. It depends on how serious the problem is and what you want to accomplish. With your family, the challenges may never be serious enough to warrant a formal meeting. And even if they are, you may be able to accomplish what you want with less formal communication. Use whatever works. But regardless of the format you want to use, you will be more successful if expectations are clearly delineated and written down (our memories sometimes aren't that good!), as well as consequences for unacceptable behavior. In addition, if you do not have some kind of planned follow-up, you are not likely to see the results you hope for.

Q You make it sound easy to control one's temper and to speak in a calm, peaceful way when you are talking with an adult child about things that could destroy her soul. How can we even think about being calm when there is so much at stake?

A That's the Savior's way, and it's the way that works. But you will probably need His help to do it. Fortunately, His grace is available at such moments if we will seek it and humble ourselves in the process. From a practical standpoint, angry parents tend to be both irrational and less likely to see things clearly or objectively. Their decisions, therefore, tend to be off the mark and often counterproductive. Furthermore, their anger induces a like reaction from the adult child, which further deteriorates the communication and the relationship. When there is so much at stake, you can't afford to be angry.

Q Every time my son, who is living with us, asks me to do something for him that I don't want to do, he insists that I give him a reason why I won't do it. Sometimes when I tell him that I just don't want to do it, he persists in trying to get me to give him a "better" answer. This creates friction between us, and I don't like that, but I don't think I have to give him an answer that is acceptable to him every time I won't do what he wants me to do. What do you think?

A Your son's behavior manifests an attitude of expectation rather than of gratitude. He obviously has some maturing to do. If you have not already done so, sit down with him and let him know that since you are the one who is doing the sharing, you have the sole right to determine when, where, and what you will share. You are not answerable to him about this and have no obligation to give him any reason for your decision. Tell him that when you feel it would be helpful for him to know the reason, you will let him know. Otherwise, you won't. Explain that his insistence on your justifying your decisions to him is hurting your relationship and that you don't want that to happen. Get his commitment to stop it.

Q I am a single parent, and I think I need to hold a Responsibility Meeting with my two children who are living at home, but I am afraid to do it. They can talk me into or out of just about anything. What would you suggest?

A If you do not feel that you can handle the situation by yourself, ask for some help. This could be from your home teacher, your visiting teacher, your bishop, your Relief Society president, or another mature adult member of your family, like a brother, father, or mother. Sit down with them and plan out the Responsibility Meeting using the guidelines we have given, then have them be in attendance at the meeting. You should conduct, but they can lend moral, emotional, and even physical support, as needed. They should never play the role of mediator, however. They are there to support you and your decisions. Your situation will only get worse if you do not get this out on the table and resolved.

Q Our returned-missionary son who lives with us goes to R-rated movies. We have spoken to him about this in casual conversations, but have only expressed our disapproval. Do you think this is serious enough that we should hold a Responsibility Meeting with him?

A Yes. One of the purposes of Responsibility Meetings is to help prevent serious future problems. His behavior itself is contrary to the counsel given to us by every recent prophet and is likely a violation of the covenants he has made in the temple. This habit will lead him to even greater virtue challenges if he doesn't stop it now. A carefully planned Responsibility Meeting, conducted by the Spirit, may be exactly what he needs to become aware of the danger of his present path. Remember to present your concerns and your expectations, have a frank two-way discussion, then come to decisions that are acceptable to you, and hopefully to him. You will bless his life by doing this.

Q I am a single mom with two young children. I invited my adult son and my adult daughter to live with me. They refuse to contribute to rent or to food and won't even talk to me. How can I hold a Responsibility Meeting with them?

A You might not be able to, but that doesn't mean you can't communicate what you expect of them and the consequences if they don't meet those expectations. Go ahead and plan your meeting and write up an agenda. Give them a copy, indicate the time of the meeting, and tell them that it is important for them to be there. Tell them that you are going to make decisions at that time that will affect them, whether or not they are there. Be kind, but be firm. Hold your meeting, with or without them. Make your decisions, then stick to them. If necessary, get help from someone outside to enforce your decisions. This will be difficult for you in the short run, but it will be best for all concerned over the long haul.

Q My son and his wife have borrowed a substantial amount of money from us and want to borrow some more. They have been sporadic in their payments for the last loan, and we are reluctant to loan them any more money. I asked them to come and talk to us about it, but my son won't do it. His wife said she is willing to meet with us, though. Should we go ahead with a Responsibility Meeting with just her?

A Your meeting will not be as effective unless both of them are there. You should try very hard to get him to attend with her. You might consider telling him that you will make no decision on another loan until he meets with you. If you are willing to consider a future loan if certain conditions are met and you want to discuss this with just your daughter-in-law, go ahead. You should have a written agenda, though, and write out your decisions so that neither your son nor his wife will have any questions about your expectations and requirements.

Q We want to hold a Responsibility Meeting with our daughter (and need to!), but we are concerned that the formality of that meeting will turn her off. Should we hold it anyway?

A Yes, but you may want to modify it so that it will work for you. For example, if an opening prayer is not feasible, you and your wife should pray before meeting with your daughter. Don't label it a meeting—just tell her you would like to talk with her. You should still plan out ahead of time what you want to discuss with her, and then follow that agenda just as though you had written it out. Afterwards, you should write down what you have decided and give a copy to your daughter so that there will not be a misunderstanding.

Q How important is it to have follow-up meetings after you have held a Responsibility Meeting? That seems to be overkill to me.

A The important thing is that you follow up to make certain your expectations are being met, do it when you say you will, and make modifications in your previous decisions that you feel are appropriate. If you are not doing this, you have negated the whole purpose of the Responsibility Meeting. You will send a clear message that you will not hold your adult child responsible. A follow-up meeting is one way to have this accounting. You may prefer a less formal way. Use whatever works for you, but follow up.

CHAPTER 10

YOU CAN'T LEAD WHERE YOU'RE NOT GOING

Principle 10: The righteousness of parents dramatically affects both the rightness of their decisions and how those decisions will ultimately influence their adult children.

Lenore watches as the bishop marries her daughter, Sandie, and Sandie's boyfriend, Duncan. Sandie has just turned eighteen and has been living with Duncan for the last six months. Lenore wonders how all of this could be happening. Sandie went to seminary the previous year and was going to church faithfully. All of her friends were good Mormon girls. Lenore urged Sandie not to be unchaste and to wait until she was older and had some schooling before she got married. Sandie has never been rebellious or uncooperative, but she would not listen to any of the counsel that Lenore had tried to give in this situation. In fact, she has told Lenore that she really doesn't want to be involved in the Church.

After the ceremony, Lenore talks to her home teacher, Brother Schmidt, who has attended the wedding. She has been on the phone with him a number of times in the past few weeks. She tells him that she hopes Sandie will be okay and that she wishes Sandie had made some different choices. She can't figure out why Sandie has done what she has done. Brother Schmidt nods in agreement, but doesn't say anything. He thinks back over the past year that he has been Lenore's home teacher.

Lenore has been receptive to him as a home teacher, but has been inactive in Church and was unresponsive to his invitations to attend Church. Lenore has never married (Sandie was born out of wedlock), but she lived with Sandie's father in Washington up until three or four years ago. That relationship ended, and Lenore moved down to southern California with Sandie. Lenore came to some of the ward socials, and Brother Schmidt was instrumental in getting Sandie to attend seminary. Lenore continually expressed her "testimony" of the gospel, yet she always seemed to have an excuse for not coming to church. She was usually too tired to read the scriptures and did not want to accept a Church calling. When Sandie started to turn away from the Church and its standards, Lenore asked Brother Schmidt to try to talk some sense into Sandie. He had several conversations with her. She was polite, but unreceptive to his counsel. He wondered if things would have been different with Sandie if Lenore had shown more interest in internalizing the teachings of the Church and bringing Sandie to church rather than sending her. Unfortunately, Lenore didn't set a righteous example for her daughter to follow.

Parents have the *sacred responsibility* to help their adult children know how to be happy by *showing* their children how to be happy through the way they are living their own lives. In fact, we, as parents, are commanded to "bring up [our] children in light and truth," and we are admonished to "teach them to walk in the ways of truth and soberness; [and] . . . to love one another, and to serve one another" (see D&C 93:40; Mosiah 4:15). We cannot meet these parental responsibilities without setting an appropriate example, and these obligations apply regardless of the age or status of the children. Families and parents are forever, and there is no time limit with respect to this nuclear parenting responsibility to be a Christlike example to our children.

While it is not true that a "bad" parent always has "bad" children or that a "good" parent always has "good" children (remember the agency principle), it is true that parents who are *striving* to live the kind of life they expect or *hope* their children will live are more likely to see their expectations realized. Why? Because parents who try to follow the Savior receive the fruits of those efforts, which are peace, joy, and guidance by the Holy Ghost. In addition, they open the door for the Savior's grace, which brings them strength and wisdom beyond their own. These gifts, in turn, will bless their adult children as well.

Parents who live less than faithful lives send wrong, even potentially destructive, messages to their children. The "do as I say, not as I do" lesson that is taught certainly does little to foster a sense of morality or responsibility in the adult child. In fact, it is more likely to bring added disrespect for the parent and a subsequent disregard for just about any counsel the parent may give. Worse still, the adult child may pattern his or her own behavior after such a model. Rather than parents receiving revelation to lead their children to the light of the gospel, "light and truth" may actually be kept from those children because of the sinful actions ("traditions") of their parents (see D&C 93:39).

In addition, parents' less-than-acceptable lifestyles impede them from doing the right or best things for their children. Such parents can become a significant part of an adult child problem and are not likely to be of much help in the solution of that problem until, or unless, they are willing to get their own lives in order. The sins of the children may very well be on the heads of such less-than-faithful parents as a result (see 2 Ne. 4:5–6).

Parents whose lives bear testimony of the reality of Jesus Christ and of His Atonement give their children the greatest gift, outside of life itself, that they can bestow upon them. They literally *show* them who they are and show them the path that will lead them to peace and fulfillment on this earth. In the words of Elder Robert D. Hales of the Quorum of the Twelve Apostles, "[Parents] *assist* [the Lord] in reaching [their children who have strayed] by faithfully living the gospel, being sealed in the temple, and living true to the covenants [they] make there" ("With All the Feelings of a Tender Parent: A Message of Hope to Families," *Ensign*, May 2004, 91; italics added).

PARENTAL RIGHTEOUSNESS BRINGS PARENTAL RIGHTNESS

Righteous parents are entitled to receive divine guidance as they seek to bless their adult children. There is a direct relationship between a parent's proximity to the Savior and his or her ability to *understand* what the Lord is trying to tell that parent about how to help an adult child. When Jesus Christ was ready to appear to surviving Saints on the American continent following His Resurrection, God the Father announced His arrival in a "small voice." At first the Saints who were gathered at the Bountiful temple knew that someone was speaking, but they could not understand what was being said. The voice spoke three times before the Saints "did open their ears to hear it." The voice never raised; it continued still and small, though it pierced those who heard it to "the center." It was the responsibility of the Saints gathered at the temple to prepare themselves to hear it and to understand it (see 3 Ne. 11:1–7).

Perhaps the Lord is constantly sending out by His Spirit specific instructions to us parents regarding what we need to be doing to help our adult children, but we often do not hear what He is saying. It is like we are immersed in spiritual radio waves, but our radio is not turned on, nor is our antenna up so we can pick up and discern the signal. Our righteousness makes us *spiritually sensitive*. It turns on our radio and raises our antenna to receive the spiritual instruction God is giving us. Elder Neal A. Maxwell has said, "Personal revelation regarding parenting can provide customized guidance and reassurance" ("Take Especial Care of Your Family," *Ensign*, May 1994, 90). That revelation comes as we sensitize ourselves to the Spirit and as we *ask* for it. The following story is an example of what the Lord can and will do if we ask for it.

Pat and his wife, Jan, had been overwhelmed with the challenges they were having with their daughter Marilyn. Marilyn had been married and divorced; she had one son from that marriage. Pat and Jan had been given custody by county social services of Marilyn's son when he was less than two years old because of Marilyn's negligence. For two years they raised him, then let custody revert back to Marilyn because she seemed to be getting her act together. Marilyn remarried and had two more children. Things appeared to be stable, but they weren't. Marilyn and her husband divorced, and Marilyn found herself out on her own again without any way of supporting her children.

Pat and Jan did everything they could to help her. They rented an apartment for her, then arranged for her to take cosmetology classes. They provided babysitting for her children while she attended school. The situation rapidly deteriorated, however. Marilyn stopped going to school and began to party like she did before she was married. The children were often left alone to fend for themselves, with the seven-year-old literally taking the responsibility of being a parent to his two stepsiblings. He would feed them, dress them, and get them ready for bed.

This was nearly unbearable for Pat and his wife. They knew how difficult it had been to get custody of their grandson before and didn't think the state would easily turn the custody of the children over to them. They knew also that Marilyn depended on the welfare payments she was getting for the children to keep herself going and would fight relentlessly any move that would stop that income.

In his frustration and tears, Pat begged his Heavenly Father for some answers. He lay down on his bed, picked up the Book of Mormon, and turned to where he had left off reading the night before. He was in the book of Mosiah, the fourth chapter. As he read verse 6, the words "put his trust in the Lord" leapt off the page and burned into his soul. It was as though the Lord was speaking directly to Pat through the Book of Mormon, telling him to trust Him and not worry about the problem so much. There were no specific answers given to his problem, but the Lord, in that moment, revealed to him that He was aware of Pat and Jan and of their desires to bless their daughter and protect their grandchildren. He was telling Pat that everything would be all right. A great peace flooded over him, and he slept soundly that night for the first time in a number of days.

Within the next few weeks, Marilyn announced that she wanted to go live in another state. Pat and Jan told her that they would take the children if she wanted them to while she got herself situated. Marilyn jumped at that offer. She even consented to giving them legal custody. For the time being, the children would be safe. Pat wept.

Of course, it isn't just our righteous living that opens the door to revelation. It also requires our steady immersion in the word that God has already revealed (or is revealing) to His prophets and others. His word is found in the scriptures, in the utterances of modern-day apostles and prophets, and in the ordinances of the temple. It is found in sacrament meeting talks and priesthood and Relief Society lessons. It is not a coincidence that Pat found his answer in the scriptures. Parents who consistently avail themselves of God's word will find that God will most often answer their petitions for revelation regarding their adult children *through the words He has already revealed.* This is no less revelation and no less personal to us than if an angel appeared and gave us a list of "to-dos." It is likely, furthermore, that parents who take these things "lightly," and who do not avail themselves of the specific spiritual guidance they offer, will find themselves condemned (see D&C 84:54–58)—at least condemned in the sense that they have cut off the Lord and His revelations to them, revelations that are necessary if they are to bless their children as they are capable of doing.

The promise "ask, and ye shall receive" is real and efficacious (see D&C 4:7). Righteous parents are entitled to the promptings of the Holy Ghost as they seek to do what is right for their adult children. This revelation comes as a result of *seeking* it. Seldom is it a unilateral process. The "asking" is an act of humility that rends our veil of pride, allowing God's revelatory light to seep through to our hearts and minds. As we strive to make ourselves capable of hearing and understanding what the Lord would tell us, by living righteously and pondering words He has already revealed, we have the promise that the Holy Ghost will be our "constant companion" (see D&C 121:46).

APPENDIX TO SECTION 1

PARENT BYLAWS YOU CAN LIVE WITH

These are the ten parenting principles that cannot be overlooked if parents are to bless and be blessed in their sacred parental responsibilities to their adult children:

1. Parents never outlive their responsibility to their children.
2. Parents and children have the ability and the right to make choices independent of the others' decisions and actions.
3. Positive change generally does not occur until parents allow their children to experience the consequences of bad decisions.
4. The Savior's way is the only one that ultimately works. His motivation is love; His technique is invitation.
5. Appropriate parental flexibility and patience enhance the "growing-up" process.
6. Our time is usually best spent looking for solutions to challenges rather than for who is to blame.
7. Parental decisions regarding any member of the family will affect every other member. Where the family's finite resources are used is usually an either/or choice.
8. Choosing to be happy brings peace and increases parents' ability to deal effectively with adult children.
9. Parents who seek to communicate frequently, accurately, and lovingly with their adult children are likely to see relationships improve and their children behave more responsibly.
10. The righteousness of parents dramatically affects both the rightness of their decisions and how those decisions will ultimately influence their adult children.

These principles are more intuitive than revelatory. In a sense, we are just reminding you of truths that you have heard throughout your life. Hopefully, though, seeing these principles in the context of dealing with your adult children will help you apply them more effectively and consistently as you seek to carry out your sacred parental responsibilities. Be patient with yourself. Be willing to change some things you are doing, if need be, and then let time work on your side.

To assist you in remembering these truths, we have created the following parent bylaws. Put them where you can see them and strive to apply them. They work!

I   I will remember my eternal responsibility to be a parent.

II   I will do whatever I can do for my adult children as long as they do whatever they can do for themselves.

III   I will respect my children's right to make choices, and I expect them to honor my right to do the same.

IV   I will take full responsibility for my actions and insist my children take full responsibility for theirs.

V   I will love my children.

VI   I will exercise patience and compassion according to the experience and understanding of each child.

VII   I will not be involved in unwarranted self-blame.

VIII   I will not allow any child to detrimentally affect my marriage or any other family member.

IX   I will not give beyond my ability to give.

X   I will choose to be happy.

XI   When necessary, I will use extended family, spiritual leaders, and friends to help me.

XII   I will make good communication with my children a priority.

XIII   I will strive to live a Christlike life.

XIV   I will listen to the Spirit.

XV   I will do my best, then seek the grace of Christ to do the rest.

XVI   I will not sacrifice my peace.

XVII   I will never, ever, ever give up on any child.

SECTION 2

LET'S GET PRACTICAL—APPLYING THE PRINCIPLES

To not apply what we have learned through life's experiences and observations is to waste our mortal probation. To seek to apply knowledge humbly and righteously is to follow in the footsteps of God.

CHAPTER 11

DEALING WITH IT

You may be among those few parents whose relationships with all of their adult children are everything that they should be, and there are just no significant challenges worth talking about. Chances are, though, you have either had some "hiccups" in your relationships or have some now. That's probably why you are reading this book.

The purpose of this section is to give parents who are having taxing problems with their adult children some specific suggestions as to how to apply the Ten Parenting Principles. The following chapters focus on particular difficulties that likely will strain parent–adult child relationships. While we are not offering any formulas that automatically bring about a desired relationship or result (there aren't any!), it is likely that the examples and counsel given in these chapters will help parents better manage their individual hard-to-handle challenges with their adult children. We hope so.

However, before moving on to the chapters that deal with your specific problems, we strongly suggest you evaluate your own unique challenges using the systematic steps outlined in this chapter. Obviously, if a situation is not *perceived* as a problem, the process stops. While sometimes it is absolutely clear that there is a problem, there are other times when it is not so cut-and-dried. In essence, you need to decide if a situation is unacceptable *to you*. Once that is done and it is determined that a problem exists, you should proceed to assess it. An objective evaluation will help you see your situation in "context." That, in turn, will allow you to ultimately make those decisions which will most likely be a positive step forward, given your own peculiar set of circumstances.

STEP 1: DEFINE THE PROBLEM

To know or even to feel that a problem exists is one thing; to know what the problem is, is another. Focusing on a nonexistent issue, or just on the symptoms of a difficulty, is stressful and nonproductive. More important, it can exacerbate the challenge and create parent-child schisms that are not easily repaired. Needless to say, defining the problem as specifically and accurately as possible is a critical step in getting it resolved.

How do you go about doing that? Here are some questions that may be helpful in that process:

- What problems seems obvious?
- Will our understanding of the problems be increased by talking to our child? (This needs to be done carefully, tactfully, and without accusation. At this stage it is primarily fact finding. Doing something about it comes later.)
- Will our understanding of the problems be increased by talking to those who are close to our child? (Care needs to be taken to maintain confidentiality and to avoid alienating the child with reports coming back that his or her parents are "spying.")
- What does the Spirit say?

How severe is the problem? The severity of any problem with an adult child is mostly subjective. It has much to do with the perception of the parents, which is affected by their own past experiences; their mental, emotional, and physical well-being; and their spiritual status and maturity. There is no set standard, therefore, that can be utilized to measure the severity of a problem. However, most certainly, the degree of possible harm (physical, mental, emotional, and spiritual) that could be potentially inflicted upon the adult child and other members of the family, as well as the timing and future impact of that harm, say much about the severity of the problem. That, in turn, will dictate the content and quantity of parental resources that will be used to try to bring the situation to an acceptable resolution.

Determining the nature and severity of challenges we have with our adult children *before* we begin to try to do something about them will almost surely increase the effectiveness of our efforts. It will reduce the likelihood of getting on the wrong road and the frustration that comes when we discover our error after we are well on our way.

STEP 2: DETERMINE IF WE CAN DO SOMETHING ABOUT IT

Of all communications between astronauts in space and mission control, the statement that is most likely to make the technicians on earth break out in a cold sweat is, "Houston, we have a problem!" Their concern is not so much finding out what the problem is (they are virtually certain they can do that) as getting it taken care of. There are things mission control can do to solve problems themselves without the aid of the astronaut. Often, however, a problem lies either with the astronauts or their ship. Mission control, therefore, is frequently left in a state of helplessness. They can give instructions, but the astronauts need to perform the correcting action. If it is to be done, the astronauts must have both the ability (the knowledge, skill, and physical, emotional, and mental capability) *and* the willingness to do it. All mission control can do is wait to see if and how the astronauts respond. They know that the lives of the astronauts are hanging in the balance.

The analogy between "Houston, we have a problem!" and parents coping with a problem with their adult child is obvious. What makes the parental challenge even more difficult is not only that the problem may be exacerbated by the child's unwillingness to cooperate, but that the unwillingness may be the problem. Most certainly, given the agency principle, what, if anything, parents can do to meaningfully help their child is almost completely determined by that child's willingness to receive the help and to do something about his or her problem.

So the question, "Can we do something about it?" is a legitimate one that all parents faced with these issues must ask. And the more objectively and thoroughly they answer the question, the more significant and workable will be their ultimate plan to deal with their problems with their adult child.

In some instances no analysis is necessary, for it is clear that parents can do little or nothing about the problem. Such circumstances are rare and usually involve children who have either severed all contact with their parents or who are on their own and have rejected all reasonable counsel and assistance the parents and others have offered to date. Here are a few questions parents will probably want to ask to help determine if they can do something about their adult child's problem:

- Will the child sit down with you and talk, even if the conversation is strained?
- Does he or she love you?
- Does he or she currently rely upon you for assistance of any kind (such as room and board, financial, automobile, job, or transportation)?
- Can you provide additional resources to the adult child that you are not currently furnishing?
- Are there other responsible people to whom he or she will listen?
- Does the Spirit say you can do something about this?

If the answer to any of these questions is yes, then it is probable that the parents can do something about the problem. In most instances, parents can do something. While the effectiveness of what they do is largely determined by the receptivity of the adult child, objectively and thoroughly considering what is possible to do will help them ultimately deal most meaningfully with the situation.

STEP 3: DETERMINE IF WE WANT TO DEAL WITH IT

On the surface, this step seems almost absurd. Why wouldn't parents who love their children want to help them when they have a problem? There are actually at least three possible reasons why they wouldn't. The first, in our opinion, is not legitimate; the second may be; and the third usually is.

1. *Parents are absolved of any responsibility to deal with their children's problems when the child becomes an adult.* This argument has been discussed in detail in the first chapter of this book. We answer it here by reiterating the first parenting principle: *Parents never outlive their responsibility to their children.*

2. *Parents are too exhausted from previous, unsuccessful efforts.* There is most certainly a sense of frustration and futility associated with trying to deal with either a chronic or acute behavioral problem with an adult child, particularly when there appears to be no positive response on the part of the child after much parental effort. It is legitimate to question whether such effort should continue or a new effort begin when another problem arises with the same child, especially when the emotional, physical, and mental state of the parents might be threatened. In any case, the ultimate decision whether to continue with overt effort needs to be made with contemplation of the fifth parenting principle: *Appropriate parental flexibility and patience enhance the "growing-up" process.* Sometimes it is our own inflexibility and intolerance that brings on our unmanageable stress. To cease our efforts to help our children when it is our impatience that is getting in the way will probably magnify our own stress and cause us to withhold from our children assistance they may need. We need to be careful here.

3. *The cost is too great.* Parents pay a price when they devote resources, including time and energy, toward solving the problems of any adult child. The seventh parenting principle must *always* be considered in determining what, if anything, should be done to assist a struggling child: *Parental decisions regarding any member of the family will affect every other member. Where the family's finite resources are used is usually an either/or choice.* If the allocation of time and resources to solving the problem of an adult child will be *unacceptably* detrimental or neglectful to the rest of the family, or any member of it, then it probably should not be done.

While parents should never rationalize away their involvement in their adult child's challenges, there are sometimes legitimate reasons for either curtailing that involvement or eliminating it. Relying upon the Spirit for guidance and honestly evaluating our own motivations will help us know when this action should be taken.

STEP 4: COME TO A PARENTAL CONSENSUS

It should be obvious that agreement between parents is something that should be happening at each stage of this process of problem evaluation. If both parents are seeking the Spirit and are sensitive to one another, parental consensus will almost be automatic. It is not expected, and it is *not necessary*, that complete agreement be reached concerning every detail and nuance of a problem with an adult child. However, it is essential that there be basic parental agreement that there is a problem and about what the nature of the problem is. While there may be some disagreement about the relative severity of the problem between the parents, there needs to be consensus that they as parents are capable of doing something about the problem and are willing to do so. As we have discussed previously in this book, the effectiveness of any approach to solving a problem depends on the degree of parental agreement. In fact, severe disagreement between parents concerning key issues will not only undermine any constructive efforts to help an adult child, but it can put the marriage and the family itself in jeopardy.

What if we cannot agree? If parents are in substantial disagreement over key aspects of their adult child's problem, they have four options:

1. Proceed unilaterally and without the other parent's blessing to try to deal with the problem.
2. Proceed unilaterally with the other parent either ambivalent or weakly disagreeing, but willing to give his or her "okay" to go ahead.
3. Stop the process altogether and neither one do anything more about the problem for now.
4. Agree to disagree relative to key perceptions concerning the problem, but be willing to compromise regarding possible actions and be united in ultimate efforts.

Option 1 is an invitation for chaos and family schisms that should be avoided except in the most extreme conditions, such as when the physical safety of the adult child or another family member is in jeopardy or when criminal behavior is involved.

Option 2 does not often work well. While the ambivalent or disagreeing parent is not actively opposing his or her spouse's actions, the potential positive impact of those actions is nonetheless diluted. This is generally a weak alternative, but sometimes it is better than doing nothing at all.

Option 3 may be the only choice if disagreements are intense and there is no hope of compromise. Postponing parental action (which in itself is an action) may be the "right" decision in such cases, both to preserve the husband-wife relationship as well as to give the situation time to germinate. If this is the decision, parents must not blame one another if the child's problem worsens.

Option 4 is usually the best course of action when disagreements exist. The fact that parents are willing to use this option usually reflects a humility and spiritual submissiveness on the part of both that will ultimately lead to the "right" things being done. Outside advice from respected individuals should be sought jointly. A third (or fourth) objective opinion can often help. If such outside counsel supports one parent's views, it should not be used as leverage to force the other parent to conform, however. Each parent is always entitled to his or her view, and that view needs to be respected by the other.

Usually, severe disagreements between parents can be resolved through a willingness on the part of both to be conciliatory, respectful of each other's opinions, and willing to seek the Spirit for guidance. Only in the most exceptional of circumstances is one parent justified in proceeding with a course of action without the full support and consent of the other.

SUMMARY

Without careful, meaningful evaluation of a perceived problem with an adult child, it is highly unlikely that concerned parents can deal with it effectively or deal with it in a way that will be least disruptive to themselves and other family members. Sometimes it can be a significant process just to determine if a problem even exists. But that determination doesn't carry with it an automatic solution to the difficulty. Only after giving thought and effort to defining the problem, making a determination that we can do something about it, and deciding that we want to do something about it, are we actually ready to proceed with the formulation of a plan to deal with that issue. Perhaps the most critical aspect of an ultimately successful plan is having both parents work in tandem. If there is not consensus, or at least cooperation and accommodation between the spouses, virtually any plan is doomed.

As you strive to apply the ten parenting principles, this systematic approach to problem evaluation should help you in handling the unique challenges you are having with your own adult children. But, as we have suggested throughout this book, your greatest aid will be the Spirit. Good luck!

QUESTIONS & ANSWERS

Q Our daughter is doing some strange things, like going into her room whenever she's home and locking the door and sometimes not coming out for hours. She never used to do this. She also hardly ever seems to have any money. She went to college for a year after high school but didn't do that well and has been working for the last year. She doesn't have that many expenses, so I don't know what she's doing with her money. I think there's a problem here, but my wife doesn't. What do you think I should do?

A First, invite your wife to sit down with you to talk with your daughter about your concerns. Assure her that the conversation with your daughter will be nonthreatening, and be specific in suggesting what you would discuss with your daughter. Ask your wife what she thinks should be said. If you are in agreement, then meet with your daughter. If your wife is not willing to participate, ask her how she would feel if you met with your daughter. If she doesn't feel okay about it, *and you feel that your daughter is not in imminent physical danger,* it is probably best that you do not go ahead with that meeting at this time.

Q Our returned-missionary daughter has been involved with some boy in an Internet romance for the last three or four months. He is not a member of the Church, and our daughter says she hasn't discussed the Church with him other than to tell him she went on a mission. They have moved from the Internet to the telephone, and the monthly bill is extremely high, since he lives several thousands of miles away. Our daughter pays her share of the bill, but my wife and I think there is a problem. My wife thinks the situation is a lot worse than I do, though, and wants to ban our daughter from the phone and the computer. I think that will push her away from us and cause more trouble than exists now. I feel like I'm caught between my wife and my daughter, and I don't want to hurt either one of them. Help!

A If you have not already done so, you and your wife should have a frank talk with your daughter about your concerns. If after that conversation neither you nor your wife feel differently about the severity of the problem, you should strive for a compromise that is acceptable to both of you. For example, you may want to consider just limiting your daughter's time on the computer and phone for a month or two, then taking a look at the situation. In any case, this doesn't warrant potential alienation between you and your wife.

Q I am married for the second time, and we are a bit older. My husband has a troubled forty-year-old son who moved in with us (into *my* nice home) the day after we got home from our honeymoon. He is not married and has a lot of bad habits. I don't like him there, but my husband says we can't kick him out because he is his son. What do you think?

A We wish we could push a magic button and solve this one. The button we would push is the one on the telephone to call the moving van to come and get him. This is not fair to you or to your marriage and needs to be addressed. We suggest that you talk to your husband and explain to him how important it is to you that his son does not stay. If needed, have your bishop counsel with him. If your husband still insists that his son stay, then you will need to deal with it humbly but with firmness. It is not right that his son stays if you cannot live with it, and it is *your* house! You will need to make a tough decision here, and, either way you go, it may well affect your marriage.

CHAPTER 12

DIFFICULT LIFESTYLES

One of the most common challenges parents of adult children have is how to deal with an adult child who lives with them but behaves in an unacceptable manner. Here are some questions that parents should ask themselves regardless of what their child's specific inappropriate behavior might be.

- Can we, as parents, tolerate our child's behavior?
- Will the other children who are at home be negatively affected by it?
- Is putting up with the objectionable behavior of our adult child helping or hurting him or her?
- What can we, as parents, do that we are not now doing that might help?
- Are we, as parents, in basic agreement as to what to do?

These questions reiterate what we have already discussed in this book. But answering them as honestly and completely as you can will help you determine the direction you want to go as you deal with the adult child who is behaving unacceptably. In this chapter we will discuss two undesirable lifestyle types that parents deal with most frequently.

LAZY SYNDROME

One of the most common problems parents face is when adult children do nothing. True, they are not out raising Cain, but they are not out there being productive citizens either. Consider the following story as an example of lazy syndrome.

Randy comes home from his mission after serving honorably for two years. He says he wants to go to college and is willing to get a job, but he'd like to relax for a few weeks before looking for the job so he can adjust to postmission life, and school doesn't start for a couple of months anyway. His mom and dad say that's okay. Randy says he's going to need a car. His parents say they'll help him get one, but he is going to have to make the payments on it. He agrees. He gives an outstanding homecoming talk in sacrament meeting, and he looks great. Things just couldn't be better.

Six months later Mom and Dad start to worry. Randy is active in the Church but only sporadically attends young single-adult activities and does not attend institute at all. He tries several jobs but quits them after working only a few weeks at each. He makes only one car payment. His parents make the other payments, hoping that he will soon be able to get on his feet financially. Randy registers for fifteen units at college, but after school starts, he drops all but one class. He sleeps in until late in the morning, watches TV most afternoons, and is out with his friends every night. He borrows a lot of spending money from his parents, promising that he will pay them back when he gets a "steady" job. He doesn't help around the house, and his room is always messy.

His parents decide to talk with him about where he is going. He says that he is okay, that he has just needed some time to adjust, and that he's ready to move ahead now. They breathe a sigh of relief—but cross their fingers.

Six months later, it is the same story, except now Randy isn't even taking a class at college and he hasn't worked a day in the last three months. Mom and Dad decide they aren't doing Randy any favors. They have tolerated one broken promise after another. It is obvious that he is very comfortable and is going absolutely nowhere with his life. The parents talk it over between themselves and decide what they need to do. They tell Randy that they are going to have a family council (Responsibility Meeting) with him to make some decisions about his situation, and they want his input. Randy comes, the meeting is cordial, and there is an honest exchange of feelings. Randy acknowledges that he hasn't been doing what he should be doing. His parents tell him that they have done everything they know how to do to help him and have decided that the best thing for Randy right now is to be on his own. They tell him they will give him thirty days to find an apartment and that if he misses another payment on the car, they will take it back. The discussion turns disagreeable. Finally, Randy agrees that he will look for an apartment and make payments on his car. His parents tell him they will pay the first month's rent and the next month's car payment.

Fifteen days pass and nothing has happened. Twenty days go by, and still Randy has not looked for an apartment. He obviously does not think his mother and father mean what they have said. His parents call around and find an apartment for him. On the thirtieth day, his parents gather Randy's stuff together and move it to his new apartment. Randy is out of the house.

Things are not very pleasant for a while, but ultimately, in this case, it works. Randy gets a job (he has no other choice), and over time, he assumes responsibility for his life. Both he and his parents are pleased with the results.

This somewhat severe action is not always the answer to a Lazy Syndrome problem, of course, and there is no guarantee that it will bring about the desired results. But often it does. It is not a cruel act to give a son or daughter the opportunity to develop a more responsible attitude. Rather, it is an insensitive, even unwise, parent who refuses to take the hard steps that are necessary to *help* his or her adult child get on with life. All parents have a difficult time finding the fine line between enabling and aiding. But a pretty good rule of thumb to follow is this: If what I am doing is not bringing about an acceptable change in my adult child's irresponsible behavior, it's time for me to change what I am doing. While it is usually best to err on the side of leniency, parents must recognize that mercy unwisely substituted for justice will hurt their adult child.

Here are some other actions parents may want to consider as they strive to help their unmotivated adult children:

- Encourage them to get vocational counseling (e.g., LDS Employment Services).

- Charge room and board (or a portion of it) if they are not meeting expectations. Reduce the charges as they make appropriate progress.
- Charge them for having someone clean their room weekly if they will not keep it clean.
- Set parameters on their car usage. For example, limit its use to going to work or school or church until they are accepting appropriate responsibility.
- Solicit outside help (such as bishop, Relief Society president, peer, or institute director).
- Help them get organized and set realistic goals. (It may be they just don't know how.)
- Do not "loan" money. Rather, give tasks to do so they will have to earn the money you give them. Make the tasks reasonable but meaningful. Be careful to avoid assigning tasks that would be demeaning.
- Hold them to their commitments. Attach consequences to unkept commitments and follow through.
- Pray a lot! Every child is different, and parents are entitled to, and will receive, specific spiritual guidance as to what to do.

VIOLATING CHURCH STANDARDS

Though dealing with lazy adult children can be discouraging and disheartening, dealing with children who violate Church standards can be grievous. In these cases (as in all others) parents need to seek counsel and guidance from the Lord and do what they can to maintain the Spirit of the Lord in their homes. In fact, every parent has both the responsibility and the *right* to create a home environment where the Spirit of the Lord can dwell. No member of the family has a right to do anything in the home that would either eliminate or reduce that Spirit.

Parents do not need to accept or even tolerate the consistent abuse of Church standards of their adult children who are living with them. Particularly is this true of adult children who violate serious Church laws within the walls of the home itself. Such intolerable violations consist of promiscuity (including homosexual activity), vulgar music, drug use, smoking or drinking, use of bad language, reading or viewing pornography, physically or verbally intimidating other family members, and watching R- or X-rated movies, videos, or TV programs in the home. While parents need to decide *how much* they are willing to tolerate, they need to keep in mind they don't have to tolerate *any* of this if they do not want to.

So what do you do when your live-in adult child is not keeping acceptable standards? You hold a Responsibility Meeting. First, Mom and Dad get together to evaluate the problem, discuss what behaviors they will and will not accept from their adult child, and then come to a consensus. They call the meeting with their child and conduct it lovingly but firmly. Expectations are spelled out, and a commitment to abide by those expectations is requested.

How these expectations are presented is very important. It makes a difference if the adult child thinks his parents are acting arbitrarily or capriciously instead of understanding that the expectations are a direct consequence of his choices. Parents should express their love for their adult child and their desire to have him live in their home. They should tell the child that, in fact, it will be his choice as to whether he will stay. The parents need to explain that since this is their home, they have a right to determine the kind of standards that are to be maintained in their home, just as their child has the right to decide what, if any, standards he wants to live. If the child decides to live in the home, then he is deciding to stay within the parameters the parents have established, *whether he agrees with them or not*. On the other hand, if the adult child refuses to abide by those standards, he is choosing to live outside the home.

If the choice is to live in the home, parents will then need to spell out specifically just what is expected and get the adult child's agreement to do this. If the choice is to live outside the home, parents need to accept that choice, express their love, and keep contact with their child. Should parents compromise in these kinds of situations? That is entirely up to the parents and what they are willing to tolerate. It must be remembered that the allowance of a continued violation of any "major" Church standard within the home will detrimentally affect the spiritual environment in the home. However, parents may want to adjust consequences and expectations if any of the following conditions apply:

- The adult child has been making considerable spiritual progress lately.
- The adult child's behavior is not significantly disruptive to the rest of the family.
- The adult child's mental or emotional state requires professional help.
- The constant influence of the family has kept the adult child from more severe violations of Church standards.

What do parents do if their children do not live in their home and are living lifestyles that are unsatisfactory? The answer is whatever they can do—which may not seem like it is very much. To the extent the adult child is receiving resources from parents, the parents can help affect behavior by withholding or extending those resources.

But remember, whether their child lives with them or not, ultimately it will be the parents' love, prayers, and Christlike example that will have the most influence.

QUESTIONS & ANSWERS

Q Our son has been living with us for two years since returning from his mission. He is going to school locally and has a part-time job. He is trying to turn his room into a free apartment. He bought a lock for his door (he's the only one who has a key), wants us to get him his own phone line so he won't have to wait on other family members to get off the phone, and resents our asking him where he's going and when he will be home. He won't tell us whether he will be eating with us, but he helps himself to everything in the refrigerator. We want him to be part of our family, but he wants to be isolated from us. Are we wrong to expect this of him?

A You are not wrong. As long as he is living in your home and with your family, he needs to be part of the family and should expect to participate and share with the family. That means he needs to tell you (not ask for permission, necessarily) where he is going and when he will be home. He needs to plan on being with the family at dinner when he can, not have a carte blanche with the food. He needs to use the family telephone like everybody else and take the lock off his door (or at least give you a key to it). It is natural for him to want his independence, but if he wants it as bad as it sounds, he needs to find himself an apartment and pay his own way. When he is living on your dime, he needs to do what you expect the other members of your family who are living with you to do.

Q We had to ask our twenty-three-year-old daughter to find herself an apartment and move out of our home three or four months ago. She's gotten a job and seems to be doing okay. The problem is that she still has a key to our house, and she comes in all the time when we are not here and takes food, bedding, and anything else she needs—all without asking. We've asked her for her key, but when we are at home when she comes, she says she doesn't have it with her. We've asked her to stop taking our things, but she just laughs and says it's no big deal. We don't want to alienate her, but we want this to stop. What should we do?

A Change the lock to your house.

Q I understand that sometimes it is necessary to get your kid out of the house, but when do you think they are old enough for this to happen?

A Unless the problem is really grievous, you probably shouldn't seriously consider moving your child out of your house until he or she is in the very late teens or early twenties. Even then, you should feel pretty certain you are doing what is best for them. Once children have graduated from high school, they need to understand they are guests in your home and are expected to act accordingly. If they don't, and it is intolerable for you, you are within your moral and legal rights to ask them to leave.

Q Our son wants us to pay for him to go to a school out of state where some of his good LDS friends are going. Before his mission he really bombed school and can only get into a junior college until he gets his grades up. We would have to pay exorbitant tuition for him to go out of state, and we feel he should stay at home and go to college locally until he shows he is serious about school. He has been home from his mission for a couple of months and hasn't really looked seriously for a job, and that bothers us too. School starts in a month, and he is really pushing us to let him go. What should we do?

A   Sounds like you are right on. It won't hurt him to stay home for a year, and it may help him learn a valuable lesson about consequences. You may want to set some scholastic objectives for him and, if he meets them, be willing to finance his out-of-state schooling. That will give him something to shoot for.

Q   Our son is twenty-three and lives with us. He is a good kid and has an excellent job, although he hasn't had any college yet. (He keeps saying he wants to go eventually.) We helped him buy an older car that runs well, but he just got a big leap in salary and wants to buy a $30,000 car. He can afford the payments as long as he doesn't have to pay for any food or rent at our place. We feel that what he is really asking us to do is to subsidize his expensive car, and we don't want to do that. We think he should be going to college and saving his money for that instead. What do you think?

A   Clearly he is expecting you to subsidize his car. You do not have to do that if you don't want to. Consider telling him that now that he is making such good money, it is only fair that he pay for his room and board. Set an amount that is fair. If he decides to continue living with you (he may want to move out and find his own place), you might think about taking the rent money he gives you and stashing it away for when and if he decides to go to college.

Q   I am single, and my daughter is the only one left at home. She goes to school and works part time too. She seems to be doing well, and I'm happy to have her live with me. The problem is that she keeps a horribly messy room. I've tried everything to get her to be reasonable about it, but nothing works. It really bothers me. Do I have the right to expect her to keep it clean?

A Yes, although you need to consider what it might do to your relationship if you force the point. If it is something that you simply cannot tolerate, consider doing the following. Tell her *kindly* that you expect her room to be picked up. Tell her that you do not want to offend her but that this is your home and that is what you want to have happen. Give her a day of the week you expect her room to be cleaned by. Tell her if it is not clean by then, you will clean it up for her, but she probably will not like the way you'll do it. Then take several large plastic garbage bags, and on the appointed day, if the room is not clean, you pick it up. Toss all of the clothes (dirty or clean) and the shoes that are lying around in one bag, and everything else in another. Be careful not to damage or break anything, but don't be concerned about anything else. Put the bags in her closet. Each day toss anything lying around in her room in one of the two bags. She will probably get the message.

Q Why do you think that just because a young adult is irresponsible you should kick him out of the house? Let him have fun while he's young. He's going to have plenty of time to get serious.

A We are not saying that. What we are saying is that parents have the responsibility to teach their children responsibility or *they* are irresponsible. Parents can postpone the spiritual, mental, and emotional progress of their adult children by not letting them experience the consequences of consistent incautious and undependable actions. Parents love their children and want them to be happy, but that does not mean keeping them in a never-never land well into adulthood. Rather, it means helping them to see what this world is all about and teaching them how to deal with it successfully.

Q My son lives with us and doesn't go to church anymore. I know he's messing around with girls and is drinking. He may even be doing drugs. When I try to talk with him about this, he puts his arm around me and tells me that he knows the Church is true and that he will come back to it, but right now he wants to have fun. I'm afraid that if I ask him to leave my home, he'll never come back to the Church. What should I do?

A   There are several factors that you should consider as you make a decision. (1) How disruptive are his actions to you and to your household? (2) How old is your son? (3) Does he have a job or is he going to school? If his actions are disruptive, if he is at least in his early twenties, and if he is not working regularly or going to school, you should strongly consider asking him to leave your house. On the other hand, if your son's actions are more a worry than disruptive, if he is only in his late teens, and if he is making some progress with work or school, you probably need to give him a little time before doing something so drastic as removing him from your home. In this instance, there are other things you can do to help him modify his behavior, like basing your willingness to let him use your car on his behavior, for example.

Q   What do you do if you learn that your son is sleeping with his girlfriend in your home when you are not there?
A   Hold a Responsibility Meeting and specify the standards he will have to live by if he is to stay in your home. If there is another such violation, help him pack his bags. Your home is your sacred space. For your son to exhibit such disrespect for you and your home is inexcusable.

Q   I have a nineteen-year-old who is really into drugs. How can I help him turn his life around?
A   There is no pat formula here that will guarantee immediate success. It is important to realize that addiction may be involved, and that almost always requires outside help to overcome. There are some things you can do to help your child, but the ultimate decision to change is your child's to make. You need to be consistent in expressing your love and offering help. If you can afford it, you may want to offer to pay for professional counseling. In addition, there are a number of community and government sponsored programs available. Your bishop or local LDS Family Services office can direct you to those most applicable. The bottom line is that your child must want to change before anyone can really help. Stick with him, but be willing to make those hard choices that will help him.

Q What do you do about a son who has chosen a homosexual lifestyle? He is living with us and has a good job. He is cordial to us and the other members of the family, but he insists on following "his path."

A It will be helpful for you to see "his path" as actually being made up of two parts. One is his attraction for those of the same sex. No one knows exactly why that tendency exists in some, but Church leaders and many psychologists have assured us that this proclivity can be overcome *if* the individual wants that to happen. The overcoming process usually involves *long-term* spiritual and professional counseling. Your son's desire to overcome this tendency is paramount. No progress can be made until that occurs. The second part involves promiscuous activities. One can be homosexual in his or her sexual inclinations, yet morally clean if he or she is not now involved in impure activities or thoughts and has repented of any previous transgressions. Justifying immoral behavior just because one is homosexual is as illogical as justifying immoral behavior because one is heterosexual. Carnal behavior is carnal behavior, and its fruits are misery and decay. One thing you can do is to try to help your son understand this difference between a tendency and an immoral act. Should you allow him to stay in your home? That is your decision to make and should be based on his actions rather than his tendencies. The Church publishes several useful pamphlets on this subject, and LDS Family Services is particularly attuned to this challenge. Use these resources to help you. Your patience with his tendency, while not accepting of his actions, is key to your helping him.

Q My returned-missionary son has left the Church for a homosexual relationship. We still have contact. In fact, we have better communication than we have ever had. He calls and writes a lot. The calls are long and informative, and the letters are even longer. He wants to come home, but he won't come home without his partner, and I can't handle that. What should I do?

A It is possible that allowing your son to bring his homosexual lover to your home could be perceived by him *and by other members of your family* as your acceptance of his actions. Certainly, that potentiality must be taken into account as you make your decision, along with your own personal and spiritual discomfort if you were to allow your son to come home under his conditions. You do not have to compromise the spirit in your home. That is the basic rule. Perhaps a compromise would be to meet him on neutral ground, like on a joint vacation, for example. Remember, you can love without condoning. Be forthright in your feelings, and ask him to honor your concerns and standards. Meanwhile, keep the communication going.

Q Do I allow my daughter to move into my home with her live-in boyfriend if they pay rent and I really need the money? They have been living together for three years, and there are no children.

A What is it worth to you to maintain the sanctity of your home? We know of a situation where a single mother invited her daughter and the daughter's boyfriend to move in with her to help pay the rent. A year later, her second daughter asked to live in her bedroom with her boyfriend, and she would pay rent. Whatever we do, we are sending out signals. Make sure your signal is what you want to send out. We suggest you look for another renter with an acceptable lifestyle.

CHAPTER 13

PREGNANCY OUT OF WEDLOCK

Answers and solutions to situations where there is pregnancy outside of marriage aren't easy to come by, and the challenges are sometimes overwhelming. But this situation is almost always manageable if parents and involved children are *willing* to do what is right. We have seen this crisis occur a number of times, and while each circumstance is different, there are enough substantial similarities so that parents and children who are currently dealing with this challenge can learn from others who have been through it. Here is a real-life experience.

Larry (twenty-one) and Nancy (eighteen) don't know where to turn. They have been dating for over a year. She is now nearly three months pregnant. Larry has had a very rocky time of it in the past. He has made a lot of bad decisions that have kept him from going on a mission. He loves the gospel, but just hasn't been consistent in living it. He is good-natured and easy to get along with, but his parents are at their wits' end. They have done about everything they know how to do and have a good relationship with him, but they are very frustrated because they don't know how to help him.

Nancy is bright and is going to a major university away from her home. She is attractive and is well liked. Her father is a prominent Church leader in their community and is well-to-do. He has given Nancy a car and ample money to live on while she is away at school. She has missed a lot of school this semester because of morning sickness and worrying about what will happen to her, and so she dropped all of her classes. Her dad found out she dropped her classes and really lost it. And when he found out she was pregnant, he went into orbit. Finally he cooled down a bit and told Nancy not to worry about the baby and what to do with it. He told her to just tell Larry good-bye and never see him again, and they would raise the baby and take care of everything.

Nancy told her dad that she loves Larry and is going to marry him. Her dad said that if she does, she will never be a part of their family again. Then he drove to where she was living, picked up her car, and stopped sending her money. Nancy has been thrown out of her apartment because she can't pay the rent and is literally on the street. Her dad has repeated over and over again that all she has to do to get it all back is to quit seeing Larry and have nothing to do with him. Nancy is now living with Larry's parents.

When Larry's parents found out about the pregnancy they told Larry and Nancy that they will do anything they can to help. Larry was dumbfounded. He had expected to be thrown out of the house in a rage. But his parents have rallied around Larry and Nancy.

Larry and Nancy go in to see their bishop. The bishop asks Nancy some questions.

"Are you seeing a doctor?"

"Yes."

"Are you and the baby okay?"

"Yes."

"Are you out of the morning sickness yet?"

"Yes."

"Have your parents softened any?"

"Absolutely not! Perhaps they are worse than before."

"Do you have any intention of leaving Larry?"

"Absolutely not!"

The bishop then asks both of them some questions. "Do you love each other?"

"Yes."

"Do you plan to get married?"

"Yes."

"Larry, are you willing to fully assume the responsibility of being a husband and father?"

"Yes."

"Will Nancy's parents come to the wedding?"

"We can't imagine they will."

"Nancy, do you have siblings?"

"Yes. I have four sisters. The two who are married have temple marriages."

"Will any of your sisters support you in this marriage?"

"Probably not. My one sister who was very close to me is very, very angry. I don't know what they will do."

"Are you both ready to pay the price of being without the support of Nancy's parents through a marriage?"

"Yes. Without any question."

"Larry, how supportive will your parents be?"

"Very supportive. They will help in any way possible."

"Nancy, what will your parents do?"

"They will not come to a wedding. They will not do anything to help me."

After talking with the couple for another hour, the bishop gives them some counsel: "I think you need to get married as long as you love each other and want to. The marriage ought to happen soon, within a few weeks if possible. It should be a small wedding, probably at a home."

Larry and Nancy agree.

The bishop tells Nancy that she should invite her parents. She should go to see them or talk to them.

Nancy is afraid to talk to them face-to-face, but agrees to call them.

The bishop suggests she tell them that she has made some decisions and, in an adult manner, ask them for their support. She should invite them to be a part of the wedding and the plans.

The bishop tells her to let them know that Larry is the father of her baby and that he is going to be her husband and that she will not discuss that any further. The bishop suggests that Nancy tell her folks that she wants them to be very involved in their lives and that she needs them and wants to be around them, but they have to understand that she feels it is the right thing to marry Larry and she has made up her mind about that.

Larry and Nancy agree to the bishop's counsel.

COMMON PARAMETERS

Now that we have outlined Larry and Nancy's story, we want to discuss some of the common parameters that all situations like this have, as well as talk about some of the counsel given by Church leaders. We'll start with a few questions. Are Nancy's parents handling this predicament constructively? What about the way Larry's parents are handling it? What should be done differently? Should we judge them? No. But we can and should learn from what others have done. Each circumstance is unique, and the analysis of problems and the plan to confront them need to reflect that uniqueness. However, there are some commonalities, and the comments and specific suggestions below should be helpful in almost all cases.

- The official position of The Church of Jesus Christ of Latter-day Saints as stated in a June 15, 1998, letter from the First Presidency is: "Unwed parents who do not marry should not be counseled to keep the infant as a condition of repentance or out of an obligation to care for one's own. Generally, unwed parents are not able to provide the stable, nurturing environment so essential for the baby's well-being. When deciding to place the baby for adoption, the best interests of the child should be the paramount consideration. Placing the infant for adoption enables unwed parents to do what is best for the child and enhances the prospect for the blessings of the gospel in the lives of all concerned."
- Get counsel from the bishop and from LDS Family Services. LDS Family Services will review carefully and objectively with you and your child what her or his options are. LDS Family Services can be contacted directly about unwed pregnancy without going through a bishop, but it is almost always best to go through the bishop.
- LDS Family Services provides an excellent adoption program that ensures the adoption of the baby into an active LDS home.

- If birth parents love one another and are old enough and mature enough, marriage should be valued as a viable alternative. They probably should not marry if any of these conditions are lacking.
- The marriage decision belongs to the birth parents and to no one else if the birth parents are of legal age.
- If the birth parents do not marry, it is almost always in the baby's best interest to be placed for adoption into an active LDS home. This is true even if most of the parenting would have been done by the parents of the mother if the baby is kept.
- The least effective option, and usually the worst one for the baby, is for the single birth mother to keep the baby, independent of all of the other options.
- Abortion is never an accepted option except in cases of incest, rape, or jeopardy to the mother's life, and then only with careful counseling. With these exceptions, abortion is looked upon by the Church as a grievous sin.
- The birth mother and her family often bear the entire burden of giving birth to the baby. However, the birth father needs to be notified and involved with the decisions of adoption or keeping the baby. He is usually not given equal power. Disputes are handled in the courts.
- Custody of the baby is rarely given to the birth father or his family, even if the birth mother elects to put the baby up for adoption.
- The right thing is almost always done when all parties are putting the welfare of the baby as their top priority.

Finally, a word of encouragement. The following written comment was submitted by parents who have gone through this challenge: "Our unwed, teenage daughter became pregnant, and our hearts were totally broken. We went through a great deal of trauma. We thought things could not get worse. How could such a dreadful thing happen to us when we were working so hard to live the gospel in every detail? We did have a tough time going through this experience, but we have since found that a lot of parents have it much worse than we did or do. Please tell your readers to keep pulling for these children and be grateful for what most of these children really are. We put the baby up for adoption, our daughter is doing well in her recent marriage, and this trauma is mostly behind us. What has allowed us to get through this is that we just kept trying."

Enough said.

QUESTIONS & ANSWERS

Q How can you keep your life under control when your daughter announces an unwed pregnancy and she is only sixteen years old?

A You do it one step at a time. You will face some significant decisions in the next few months. You will sort out all of the problems you face, including the psychological, spiritual, and physical health of your daughter; the delivery of the baby; putting up the baby for adoption; and helping your daughter feel loved and welcome in your home as a teenager. Use the principles and suggestions we have given here. You can do it, but it will be very hard. If you do it well, you will have peace, and so will your daughter and the baby.

Q We want our daughter's pregnancy kept confidential. How can this be possible if I speak to our bishop or to the Relief Society president?

A There are bishops and Relief Society presidents who talk too much. But our experience is that almost all of them keep confidences. We can't guarantee confidential handling of your situation, but make sure they understand your confidentiality needs and go from there. They are the best people to help you through this experience.

Q I have heard of ways to send the birth mother away to another city for a time to have the baby. Is such a program available?

A Yes. In instances where it is desirable for this to happen, LDS Family Services can help arrange for a foster family who will work with the girl through her pregnancy and the birth. However, we have known of instances where the birth mother has gone through this experience staying at home, with a minimum amount of embarrassment and a maximum amount of personal growth.

Q How do I contact LDS Family Services?

A Referrals to LDS Family Services usually come through your bishop. Talk with him. You may contact LDS Family Services directly, however, if you wish. They will be listed in the white pages of your phone directory.

Q How can you advise us to adopt out one of our own flesh and blood into another family? How can that possibly be in the best interest of the baby?

A You need to do two things: (1) Find someone who did not get married but kept her baby, and look at the life of that baby from the baby's point of view. Even though the birth mother's family provides a lot of love, the young mother soon learns the baby gets in the way of social life and future marriage. The baby's grandparents soon find out that the birth mother expects them to take care of the baby, sometimes all of the time. Nobody's very happy about that, and the baby suffers. (2) Then find a family with an adopted baby and notice the difference. For this family, the baby is an answer to prayers and probably came after years of yearning for a child by the parents. Notice the difference in the time, attention, and love given to the baby. The decision to place the baby for adoption is made a lot easier if you look at it from the baby's point of view. But it is a very tough decision to make.

Q This is the second marriage for both my wife and me. Her eighteen-year-old daughter from her first marriage is pregnant, and the boyfriend is a total loser. Neither he nor his parents want anything to do with the baby. My wife and my stepdaughter want to keep the baby. Our daughter is extremely immature and has no idea what it means to be a mother. My wife says she is willing to raise the child and refuses to listen to either the bishop or me about placing the baby for adoption. We have been to LDS Family Services, and that didn't change their minds either. What can I do?

A Both you and the bishop should continue to talk to your wife and daughter. Be patient and try to be understanding of their position. Besides making this a focus of your own personal prayers, ask your wife and daughter to pray about it and mention it in your family prayers. Be careful that you do not alienate your wife. Be prepared to live with the situation if the baby lives with you, and do the best you can so that the baby will have the best possible chance.

Q Our daughter is not living with us and is only seventeen. She is six months pregnant and not married. She will be eighteen when her baby is born. She doesn't have much to do with the Church now either. She doesn't know whether she wants to marry the father of her baby but says she will not put the baby up for adoption regardless of what happens. She is not interested in living with us, either, and says she will just raise the child herself. We know that the baby doesn't have a chance if that happens. What are our options?

A Pray. Also be grateful that she didn't have an abortion. You probably do not have any legal rights at this time as to what your daughter does, but there is something you can do besides give her counsel. For one thing, try to get her in to see LDS Family Services. They can clearly and objectively present the realities of a single teenage mom trying to raise a child. Another thing you can do is give her some incentives for doing the right thing. For example, if you feel okay about her marrying the father of the baby and if you have the resources to do it, you may offer to help get them into an apartment and get them started, if they get married. Maybe the money you would have spent for a wedding reception under better circumstances could be used for this. There also may be some incentives you could give her to place the baby up for adoption. If you think this all sounds like bribery, you're right. Remember, we are talking about the life of an innocent baby here, and that needs to be the primary concern. Be careful and try not to alienate your daughter, though. If she does not get married and keeps the baby, leave some doors open so that you can possibly have some influence on the child.

Q Do you know of a situation where a birth mother or father has regretted the decision to put the baby up for adoption?

A This is usually a much bigger challenge for the birth mother than the birth father. The first few weeks and months following the decision to place the baby for adoption are very tough, and the birth mother is usually filled with doubts. The Spirit is very kind, though, and helps birth mothers a lot. There is peace once the intensity of the birth passes and the birth mother gets on with her life. She knows the baby is being taken care of and is in the best place for that care. You can be sure the birth mother never forgets the baby's birthday, though.

Q How can we be sure the adoptive family will treat our grandchild with the same love and respect that baby would get in our own family?

A We have very few guarantees in this life, but this one comes close. First of all, the screening process to determine eligible adoptive parents at LDS Family Services is intense. You know the baby is going to be placed with a worthy, loving family. Also, the birth mother often has a say in where the baby goes, although she seldom meets the adoptive mother. This we know for sure: adoptive parents *want* a child. And that counts for an awful lot. We are eyewitnesses to this process and can tell you that this concern of yours is one that you don't need to have.

Q Do adoptive parents pay the expenses of my daughter's baby?

A Yes, in most cases. Check with LDS Family Services to be sure and to see how much. Adoptive parents pay a rather substantial fee for the adoption privilege.

Q Can we keep in touch with the adopted baby after a placement has been made in another home?

A LDS Family Services will answer this question for certain. This is what we know: the birth parents and family usually do not know where or with whom the baby is placed. A letter or a picture can be exchanged in the initial months following the adoption. All communication is made through Family Services, never directly.

The caseworker from Family Services who works with the birth mother never works with the adoptive parents. Every effort is made to keep the identities of the birth parents and the baby confidential.

Q Can birth parents really put this experience behind them in later years, or do they spend a lot of time carrying the burden with them?

A The birth parent will not and should not ever forget the experience of giving life to a baby. The pain of that memory is ultimately reduced by time and by the degree of the birth parent's repentance. The Atonement of the Savior is real, and its power lifts the burden of sin from those who truly repent and come unto Him. We know of a number of individuals who have done this and who are at peace with themselves as a result. They are living normal lives and do not have prolonged pain.

CHAPTER 14

LOSS OF TESTIMONY

Bishop Jack Morton gets ready for bed after finishing a long Sunday of interviews and meetings. His phone rings, and as he picks it up he is hoping it isn't a member of his ward with another problem. He doesn't mind helping his people with their problems—in fact, he considers his call as a bishop a great blessing—he's just tired. It isn't a member of his ward this time. It is the bishop of his son's ward, calling from a thousand miles away.

After introducing himself, the bishop tells Jack that Jack's son Frank and Frank's wife have not been coming out to church for the last several months and that he just stopped by their home to see how they were doing. He relates the details of his visit with Frank and his wife, Anne. They tell him they will not be coming out to church anymore. They tell him they do not believe the Church is true, although they like its standards and are going to try to live those principles as a family. They will accept home teachers and visits from the bishop, but will not be accepting any Church callings or bringing their daughter out to church. The bishop asks them if either of their parents know about this. They say no. He asks them if they are going to tell them. Frank says, "I suppose it is inevitable they will find out sometime, but we have no plans to tell them right now." The bishop tries to find out what has happened to them and to see if he can answer any questions for them. They are polite, but unresponsive to his efforts. Frank says they have been doing a lot of studying and their minds are made up.

Frank's bishop tells Jack that he had a hard time deciding to call. He made the decision when he asked himself whether he would like to know if this were his son. He looked Jack's name up in the Church directory and placed the call. Jack tells him he is grateful that he did. Frank's bishop says he will maintain contact with Frank and Anne and will do everything he can to help them. Jack tells him thank you and hangs up the phone.

Jack sits on the side of his bed, numb. For a moment or two the impossibility of what he has heard drowns out the fact that he has just had such a devastating phone call. He closes his eyes and sees Frank as a little boy who had finished reading the Book of Mormon by the time he was baptized. He remembers the beautiful homecoming talk Frank gave at the completion of a very successful mission. He visualizes the glowing faces of Frank and Anne as they knelt across the temple altar to be sealed. The countenance of his granddaughter radiates in his mind as he envisions Anne reading her a story about Jesus. He recalls his deep emotion and gratitude as he joined with Frank's stake president in setting Frank apart as an elders quorum president. Then Jack's mind goes blank, and the reality of his phone conversation with Frank's bishop sets in. He buries his face in his hands and sobs.

As this story illustrates, sometimes there is nothing more emotionally and spiritually crushing to a faithful Latter-day Saint parent than the apparent spiritual loss of sons or daughters. The feelings of hopelessness and incredulity are overwhelming. What do you do now that you have not already done? You have taught them. You have testified to them. You have loved them. You have strived to live your life as a witness of that which you know to be true. What more can you do? You can continue doing all of this without faltering yourself. That consistency will be the single most important thing you can ever do as a parent to help your children find their way back.

You do have a right, even an obligation, however, to counsel them. This should not be a harping or chastisement, but a heartfelt parental admonition and invitation. This can be done in one-on-one conversations, by letters, or both. After Jack and his wife had several conversations with Frank and Anne to confirm what the bishop had told Jack and to find out as much detail as they could about what brought on this disaffection with the Church, Jack decided to write his son a letter. We are enclosing an edited version of that letter here to serve as an example of what kinds of things a loving parent might want to say to his or her spiritually estranged adult child.

Dear Frank,

The moment you were born and I looked upon your face, I discovered that love is infinite, its parameters only established by my own *willingness* to love. At that moment I loved you . . . intensely. . . . There was something else too. I knew that your mother and I had just been sent one of the spirits that Abraham talks about (see Abr. 3:23–24). And within the next few years I had unmistakable confirmation that I had the solemn responsibility to teach you the ways of the Lord so that you would be prepared to carry out your divinely appointed mission on this earth.

I savored the letters you wrote home from your mission. They were letters of testimony, of Spirit, and of love. I saw before my very eyes my son developing into who he was before he came here, and I was humbled and grateful that I was so intimately involved in that process.

. . . I knew that because of who you are, Satan would use every sophistry at his command to deter you, to turn you. And yes, son, he is real. I have my own undeniable witness of him. I have felt his siren call many times and have come to recognize it clearly. I knew that you would be subjected to nothing less. You have been in my prayers constantly that you would have the eyes to see and the grace to overcome everything that he would throw up against you.

. . . I have come to understand this singular truth: This earth is a *proving ground*. Ultimately, who we really *want to be* is manifest because we are able to externally justify whatever that is. If we want to be a fascist, a homosexual, a dictator, a born-again Christian, a Muslim, a Buddhist, or an atheist, we can select the set of facts that justifies that decision and subjugate or just ignore those facts that would not justify or confirm that choice. Hence, whatever we *really* want to be, we will ultimately become. We do not do this ignorantly either. There really is such a thing as the Spirit of Christ that has been given to all men to lead us to the ultimate truth that will make us free. That truth is this: We are literally children of a Divine Being and are on a journey here—a journey that will either give us the experience to realize our divine potential, or allow us to decide to end up somewhere short of that potential. To obtain the former is to absorb and seek to live *all* truth. To fall short is to be *selective* in what truth we will "know" and follow. That Spirit of Christ is a sense beyond that which we experience with our physical senses. And it is sure. It leads a man to believe in Christ because Christ *is* real. It leads a man to *full* truth—truth that our physical senses and our reasoning power with their gross limitations can only point to. To deny the existence of either this Spirit of Christ or its more comprehensive, more powerful manifestation in the gift of the Holy Ghost is to shut off our ability to even begin to scratch the surface of truth here in this telestial state. To accept that this spiritual power does what the prophets say it does is not selective truth-seeking. Rather, it is to recognize that there is an ultimate source of truth which can result in an unfettered view of truth—truth in its eternal context.

Time and time again I have seen men and women become so absorbed in their own intellect and so reliant upon their physical senses to determine for them what truth is that they gradually, then completely, shut off that Spirit. The irony is that they do precisely what they claim that those who seek faithfully to follow the Spirit do—ignore any truth around them that would contradict what they are doing and "believing." They deny that they ever had a spiritual experience (it now becomes an "emotion" at best or is forgotten altogether); that they ever had a testimony of the Savior or of the divinity of His Church (I was brainwashed!); or that the Church and the gospel were in any way involved in their happiness, peace, and joy (that was just my nature). In other words, they have become selective in their "factual" inputs to ultimately determine what they will believe (or not believe) and, consequently, what they will live. They ignore the powerful reality of previous experiences so that they can justify their present direction and lifestyle.

. . . There was a time in my life when I was involved in what I will call "peripheral concerns" about the Church. I wanted so badly for the Church to be true that I was sometimes reluctant to "hear what was out there." I remember as a young missionary reading the book *Blood Atonement and Plural Marriage,* which was an exchange of letters between Joseph Fielding Smith and his cousin who was the president of the Reorganized Church. They were debating the subjects listed in the title of the book and which of the two churches was the "real" church. I would read Joseph Fielding Smith's letter and say within myself, "All right!" Then I would read his cousin's letter and say, "Uh-oh!" Then Joseph Fielding Smith's answer, "All right!" and so on. Fortunately for me, the book ended up with a letter from Joseph Fielding Smith! But that was kind of the beginning of my testing the waters of contradiction.

Over the years I have read much about the "contraries." . . . I found that as I met these head on *in the context of my own personal experiences with the gospel and my continued desire to live my life accordingly,* these contraries ultimately confirmed the gospel truths. In some instances, my searching for a resolution brought quick answers; in others, it took a long time. In fact, I learned to set aside (*not ignore*) some of the more thorny ones. I would strive to not let them distract me from doing what I ought to be doing and living the way I ought to, having faith that they would ultimately be resolved. And they ultimately were. Now I know that when some not-easily-answered problems come up, it is just a matter of time before they are resolved. That is my testimony because that has been my experience. Because this is the case and because I know what I know, today I am much more interested in learning directly about the Savior and doing what He wants me to do than letting *perceived* discrepancies take up much of my time.

In saying all of this, I do not mean to minimize the struggle and thought that you and Anne have given to your testimony challenges. I know how real they are. My desire has been to reestablish for you the context in which you will ultimately resolve them. Do not take them out of the context of your experiences to date. Do not study them only from sources whose real intent is to destroy faith, not establish truth. Do not stop doing what has been a source of joy and peace and satisfaction for you in the past—attending church, serving, praying, reading the scriptures, attending the temple, and keeping your covenants. Do take these challenges to the Lord. Do humble yourself before Him and ask Him for the strength to overcome and for the knowledge to resolve. If you will confront these challenges in the light that you have both been given by your parents and through your experiences, my promise is that these challenges will become testimony strengtheners.

I know who you are, Frank.

Love,

Dad

THE ROOT CAUSE OF APOSTASY

In virtually every case, estrangement from The Church of Jesus Christ of Latter-day Saints *first* comes not because of a rejection of doctrine, veracity of the Book of Mormon, or the Prophet Joseph Smith, but because of a rejection of some aspects of the *lifestyle* that is integral with acceptance of the truthfulness of the restored gospel. When any one of us stops striving to live *all* of the commandments and keeping *every* covenant that we have made, we are turning ourselves over to Satan's power. The Holy Ghost leaves us in proportion to our estrangement from God's ways, and our rationalization distorts our vision so that our consciences can be placated.

As we work with our adult children who have "left" the Church, it is important, even critical, that we realize what the source of their apostasy is. Falling into "great errors" comes when we do not keep God's commandments (see Alma 31:9); letting the world invade our lives with its focus on money, power, and notoriety—thus replacing our concentration on service, consecration, and humility—often leads us to "reject the word" (see D&C 40:2). And when we treat the truth "lightly"—for example, not making attendance at the temple and the reading and searching of the scriptures and counsel of the prophets an integral part of our lives—our minds are susceptible to darkness (see D&C 84:54).

Testimonies will be reborn when, and only when, our spiritually disaffected children are willing to fully live truth, for their willingness or unwillingness to live truth either opens or closes their eyes to it (see Alma 12:9–11). We can best help them by personally setting examples of righteousness and by encouraging them to fully live the gospel principles. If they live those principles, then they will know of their truthfulness (see John 7:17).

PURSUING TRUTH

For those who *want to know*, there is an abundance of scholarly work written by faithful members of the Church to combat virtually every "significant" doctrinal or historical challenge raised by the Church's detractors. Remember that just because the "answers" are there doesn't mean that everyone will *see* them. A son or daughter who is testimony-challenged will only make progress if they *want* to. In that light we offer you the following guidelines to share with your children in helping regain a testimony:

Don't ignore the obvious. For every *potential* inconsistency in the doctrines and history of the Church, there are a hundred consistencies. Truth seekers do not ignore those consistencies while highlighting the potential inconsistency. One must question the real motivation of a man or woman who does this. The overwhelming number of consistencies embodied within the Church and its doctrine is prima facie evidence of its truthfulness. A seeker of truth will study the apparent inconsistencies in the context of the consistencies.

Don't eliminate the Spirit in your search. To admit to (or *hope for*) a source of truth beyond our own reasoning and senses will not compromise our own objectivity in a search for truth. We can be just as diligent in the use of our mind and eyes and ears while allowing *at least the possibility* that there is something beyond our own limited tools to help us find and know truth. Pray, read the scriptures (particularly the latter-day scriptures), keep the covenants, attend Church, serve, and attend the temple while searching for truth. To not open the door for the Spirit is to potentially grossly limit our ability to find truth.

Don't let a principle possess you. Pride plays tricks on our reasoning. When we take a stand, our tendency is to defend it at all costs, rather than be open to additional information that may modify our position. We just don't like to be wrong. Jacob said it best: "Let not this pride of your hearts destroy your souls" (see Jacob 2:16).

Let faith play a part. There needs to be a *hope* that the Church and its teachings are true. As Alma said: "If ye have faith ye *hope* for things which are not seen, which are true," and, "If ye can no more than *desire to believe,* let this desire *work in you*" (see Alma 32:21, 27; italics added). Without this desire or hope, there is no faith. Without faith, the truth cannot be found. Faith opens the door to knowledge from and by the Spirit. To rely solely on our senses and reason is to shut off that absolute source of truth. The result is that we are easily deceived, and truth becomes fleeting and obscure.

Seek answers from those who have your best interest at heart. The motivation and honesty of those who spend their lives churning out "information" that is designed to destroy faith is, at best, questionable. Look for help in finding answers from those who really do have your happiness and well-being as their motivation. Look for help from those who love you. Those who do not love you may intentionally mislead or delude. The fruits of relying on such sources for information are bitter indeed.

Don't be misled into thinking that the negatives you are struggling with are not widely known. The truth is that virtually all doctrinal and historical challenges to the Church out there are rehashes. They've been around in one form or another since the Restoration of the gospel. While there are some new twists from time to time, we hear the same things trumpeted again and again as if they have just come to light. The fact that all of this "stuff" has found its way to the Internet gives it the appearance of recency. But that is not so. Virtually every serious question has already been addressed in contemporary Mormon literature and by faithful Mormon scholars.

SOME OTHER DOS & DON'TS

- Don't try to schedule the process of your adult child's reconversion according to your own timetable.
- Don't gossip about the struggling child with other members of the family.
- Don't treat a spiritually challenged child with less love or attention than those who are faithful.
- Do recognize the agency of your child and respect it.
- Do include spiritually estranged children in family activities and communications.
- Do continue to talk about spiritual experiences and Church involvement as though the child still has a testimony.

- Do bear your testimony through your actions and verbally when the Spirit moves you.
- Do invite other members of your family, home and visiting teachers, and priesthood and Relief Society leaders to fast and pray with you for the spiritual welfare of your children.
- Do not give up!

QUESTIONS & ANSWERS

Q My son has joined another church. Will he be excommunicated from the Mormon Church?

A To join another church or to passively reject some of the teachings of the Church is not necessarily grounds for excommunication. However, if he requests in writing to have his name removed from the records of the Church, his priesthood leaders will abide by his wishes. Furthermore, if he is actively seeking to convince members of the Church to either leave it or to live practices that are contrary to the Church's teachings (e.g., plural marriage), Church disciplinary action is likely. In addition, if he is active in his public or private denunciation of the Church or is living a lifestyle that would, under any circumstances, warrant Church disciplinary action, his priesthood leaders may convene a disciplinary council for him.

Q My daughter and her husband both teach college and have nothing to do with the Church, although they are both members (as far as I know). They had their first child several months ago, and my wife and I want the baby to be blessed in the Church. Should we approach them about this?

A Yes, but carefully. We suggest you ask them if they would consider letting you give their baby a name and a blessing. If they say they do not want that to happen, let it drop for now. If they will allow you to do this, it can be done at home or at a Church sacrament meeting. Your daughter's bishop will coordinate the paperwork.

Q My son will not allow us to give a blessing on the food or have a family prayer while we are in his home . We don't want to offend him when he and his family come to our home and so have stopped saying grace or having prayers as a family when they are here. Is this wrong?

A It is the parents' responsibility to maintain the Spirit of the Lord in their own home. They need that Spirit, and they need to give their family the potential blessing of that Spirit. It is your lives that need to testify of the Savior and His Church; otherwise, there will not be a testimony given. You should say your blessings at mealtime and hold your family prayers, your scripture reading, and your gospel conversations. You should attend church and serve in your Church callings *especially* while your son and his family are there. Do this naturally and without embarrassment or concern.

Q Our son-in-law has joined Ex-Mormons for Jesus and continually sends us these tracts that tear down the Church. We are offended that he does this, but don't want to ruin our otherwise good relationship by telling him to stop. What should we do?

A Ask him to stop so your relationship won't be ruined. Tell him that you love him, but are offended by that literature. Explain to him your feelings about the Church and say that you would expect him to honor your choices as you are honoring his. Avoid confrontation or argument. If he won't stop, don't open the mail he sends, but write on the envelope, "Return to Sender," and have the post office return it to him. He will likely stop.

CHAPTER 15

CRIMINAL BEHAVIOR

In addition to unspeakable trauma and heartbreak, there are potentially injurious repercussions confronting parents whose adult children are involved in criminal activities. These repercussions are a result of *enabling parents* who seek to eliminate or lessen the severity of the consequences their criminal son or daughter is facing. In these instances, the parents themselves can be severely impacted and can bring about an indefinite postponement of serious change in their son or daughter. It is important for parents to realize that their actions are actually hurting their child.

ENABLING CRIMINAL BEHAVIOR IN ADULT CHILDREN

There are three main ways in which parents enable their children. They are discussed below. Consider them carefully, especially if your child is engaged in criminal behavior and you are (perhaps unknowingly) hindering his or her progress.

1. Obstructing justice. Lying or knowingly concealing facts in order to keep an adult child from criminal prosecution is not only immoral; it is illegal. It is called obstruction of justice and is an indictable offense. Take Millie's story for an example.

Millie received a phone call from the district attorney's office. The officer said he wanted to ask a simple question. He said that Millie's daughter, Florence, had received welfare payments for the last two years, claiming her eight-year-old daughter, Meg, as a dependent. The officer went on to say that Florence's former husband and father of

Meg claimed that Meg had lived with Millie during that period of time, so Florence wasn't eligible for payments. If that was the case, the officer said, Florence was potentially guilty of welfare fraud—a felony. "Has Meg lived with you, or has she lived with your daughter for the past two years?"

Millie hesitated. Her first impulse was to say that Meg had lived with Florence. She did not want Florence to go to jail. In the past, Florence had been involved in everything from drugs to petty theft, but she had never gone to jail. Over the last few months, Florence seemed to be making some progress, and Millie was hopeful that there might be a real turnaround coming. She reasoned that Florence going to jail would ruin any chance for that change to take place. Anyway, how could she let her own daughter go to jail?

But then she thought about all of the other times Florence "got away with it." She never seemed to have to face any serious consequences of her actions, and she just kept doing the same things over and over again. Even now Millie had justifiable skepticism as to whether or not Florence was really changing. She could hardly believe that she was ready to lie to keep Florence from her consequences again. She gave a deep sigh, then said, "I think we'd better talk, officer." Millie set a time to meet with the representative from the district attorney's office and hung up the phone.

It wasn't until she got off the phone that she realized that she would have been breaking the law, just like Florence, if she had lied. She would have been no better than her daughter in the eyes of the law. And, she knew, she would have been no better than Florence in her own eyes either. She thought of her husband, of her other children, and her granddaughter, Meg. What would her lying have done to them? She saw clearly that whatever would happen to Florence now could not be worse than the ramifications of her own dishonesty if she was not forthcoming with the truth.

2. *Being an accessory to criminal action.* If an adult child's criminal activity has been taking place in the parents' home, the parents are potentially subject to being charged as an accessory if they take no action after discovering that activity. Once parents learn that a crime is being committed in their home, they are legally obligated to inform authorities. Immediate corrective action should be taken by

parents to see the matter resolved. They may need to seek and follow legal counsel.

Errol, a twenty-two-year-old son, was secretly storing stolen merchandise in the seldom-used family garage. His parents knew that he'd had some brushes with the law and was probably doing things he shouldn't be, but they were completely unaware of the extent of his wrongdoing. One day, however, they opened the garage at the back of the house. They couldn't believe what they saw. After talking it over briefly, they immediately called the police. They learned that Errol was acting as a fence for stolen property and that they were technically considered accomplices! Without their quick action, the entire family would have been put at great risk.

In tolerating criminal behavior in the home, parents not only deny their lawbreaking son or daughter an opportunity to deal constructively with an extremely serious problem, but they literally become criminally associated with that offense themselves. Such parental irresponsibility must never be mistaken for compassion.

3. Promoting criminal behavior. Marv was raised in the Church by good parents who taught him correct principles. He was an Eagle Scout and prepared for and served a faithful mission. He came home, met, and married a righteous LDS young woman in the temple, and they were blessed with a beautiful baby daughter. But now Marv is in jail. He had been trafficking in drugs and was a user as well. He had been doing this for a number of years. He liked the fact that he had enough money to buy just about anything he wanted and didn't have to work too hard for it. His wife had divorced him several years before, but that didn't stop his criminal behavior. His mother pleaded with him to change, but he would just tell her that he was okay and that he loved her. Then he would rush off so he wouldn't have to complete the conversation.

He was arrested, then released on his own recognizance. That was no big deal, and he kept selling drugs. He was arrested again, and this time he went to jail. He was faced with nine felony counts, but his attorney was able to get six of them dropped. Since this was his first time "caught," the judge was open to plea bargaining and agreed to release Marv, if someone would post bail.

His mother wanted to do that, but his father felt that it would not be the right thing. He felt it important to allow Marv to see the consequences of his actions. He was afraid that if they jumped in now, their son would not be deterred the next time there was a temptation. Finally his wife agreed not to post bail.

Marv sat in jail, bothered that his parents wouldn't bail him out. He hated being there and was determined that he would not come back; he was far from repentant. Marv's dad visited him weekly, but his mother didn't come to see him for a long time. It was just too hard for her to see Marv behind bars. But she knew they had done the right thing by not posting bail. She knew that they may well have saved Marv from ultimately going to a state prison or, even worse, being murdered or suffering death from an overdose. She was discovering that letting her son experience consequences was the ultimate act of mercy. She realized that if she had enabled her son by posting bail she would have told him, in essence, "I will be there to eliminate the consequences of your actions, no matter how severe they are," and that he likely would have continued his unlawful behavior.

Enabling a criminal son or daughter is itself a crime—sometimes literally. There is far more at stake than what will happen to that child. Parents have a responsibility to protect the rest of their family, their own good name, and, importantly, the rest of society. To abrogate these responsibilities in order to soften or eliminate harsh consequences that a son or daughter may suffer as a result of his or her lawbreaking is a lose-lose situation.

HOW TO HELP

What can a parent do to constructively help a child who has broken or is breaking the law? Actually, quite a bit. But it will take much courage and much patience. Here are some suggestions:

- Make up your mind that you will not break the law for any reason, and let your child know that you won't.
- Be willing to report to the authorities any criminal activity that you are aware of, and let your child know that you will.
- Offer to help pay for professional counseling if you can afford it and if your child is willing to try it.

Monitor his or her progress. If you see substantive change in a *reasonable* period of time, continue to subsidize it. If you don't, stop it.

- Evaluate carefully and prayerfully any requests for money or other resources from a son or daughter who is or has been criminally involved. Apply these three principles: (1) Resources should be given *only* after a child has done everything he or she can do. (2) Resources should be given *only* when the likely outcome is a significant positive change in behavior and never when the outcome will likely encourage current unacceptable conduct. (3) Resources should be given *only* if doing so will not pose undue sacrifice on any other righteous member of the family, including parents.
- Love the child, and constantly tell him or her so.
- Pray for the child, and seek the Spirit for guidance as to what to do to help him or her.
- Seek help for your child and for yourself from Church leaders and others who have your and your child's best interests at heart (including other parents who are facing similar problems).
- Never give up.

This next story shows what can happen when a parent never gives up. Charlene sat across a table from her bishop. She was in the county jail, awaiting transfer to a state prison for a parole violation. Thirteen years before, she had graduated from the University of Utah as an English major. Then she experimented with drugs and was hooked. For the next eleven years she was on everything from speed to heroin and found herself in and out of prison for the crimes she committed to feed her habit. She had been "dry" for almost two years now and had been attending church regularly, but had apparently overdosed on some pain medication she was taking for a bad toothache and was picked up while driving a car under those conditions. She had been arrested and would have to spend sixty days in prison as a result of the violation. Charlene and the bishop both knew that this incident was an anomaly. Charlene was changing, and this would likely be the last time she would ever be behind bars.

Charlene told the bishop about her family. Her father died when she was only eight. Her mother raised her and her five siblings by herself. She took them to church every Sunday, held family home evening every Monday, had family prayer every night and morning, and read scriptures as a family on a regular basis. She said her mother could not have been a better, more inspiring parent. She said her mother was now a temple ordinance worker and put Charlene's name on the temple roll every week. "She is the most powerful example of righteousness and love, and I want to be just like her," Charlene said. "She never, ever gave up on me."

Charlene seems to be well on her way "back." And while Church leaders and good friends have certainly played a role in her progress, it is the undeviating commitment, love, and example of her mother that has been her transcending light. That example and that consistency in giving love may be all a parent can do for a child who has fallen so far. It is often enough.

QUESTIONS & ANSWERS

Q My forty-year-old son and his druggie friends break into our house every time we leave town. We have changed the locks on all our doors, so he breaks the windows. We have largely reduced our leaving town to a bare minimum, but he always knows when we are gone, even if we don't tell him. We don't have much left to steal, but he keeps coming. What do we do?

A If you know for certain it is your son who is breaking in and you can prove it, notify police, press charges, and have him arrested. For further protection, consider a burglar alarm or a security service if you can afford it. In addition, ask your neighbors to watch your home while you are gone and have them call the police if your son shows up. You might want to leave with them a statement you have signed and notarized stating that your son does not have permission to enter your home.

Q I have never been in jail other than to visit. It looked horrible. Isn't there some risk in allowing our kids to stay in jail if we have the power to get them out?

A   Maybe so, but you also need to consider the risk you run in having your child continue on a path that might lead him or her to an extended stay in jail if he or she doesn't have to suffer the consequences of his or her actions now. You are right; jail is horrible. Seeing that is often a strong deterrent to a child who is just experimenting with unlawful behavior. Remember that the law of the land is designed to protect society. If your child has done something for which the law requires him or her to go to jail, that is probably what he or she ought to do.

Q   What do you do if you find that drugs are being dealt from your home?
A   Call the police and report it. You are potentially an accomplice if you do not. You should keep this in mind: Your son or daughter is helping to ruin the lives of all of those he or she sells to. If you let this continue, you have to share in some of that blame.

Q   My son is in jail again. I am so mad at him for putting my family through this mess all of the time that I don't want anything to do with him anymore. I haven't visited him in jail since he was arrested several months ago. Do you think I'm a bad parent if I don't go to see him or have any communication with him?
A   Not necessarily. It depends on your reason for staying away from him. If it's because you are angry with him and want to somehow pay him back for what he is doing to you and your family (it's called revenge!), then you ought to rethink this—even repent. If it's because you want him to see the consequences of offending you and your family, then maybe you are doing what you should be doing. If this is the case, you should let him know that. You should tell him that you love him and that you want him to be part of your family, but when he does what he has been doing, neither you nor anyone else in the family wants to associate with him. You probably should not cut off contact altogether, though. You might consider writing him letters from time to time, even visiting him once in a while.

Q   My daughter was arrested because some of the people she was with got into a fight with some ethnic people who were at the same bar that she was at. The police called it a "hate crime," and she is facing potential time in the penitentiary. She has been in jail for two months awaiting trial, but the trial keeps getting postponed. Her lawyer says this could go on for another six months or more. We can get her out on bail, but we will have to mortgage our house to do it. I don't think she was that involved in the actual fighting, and she seems to be sorry for what's happened. What do you think we should do?

A You know your daughter and will be the best judge as to what will be the best thing for her and for you. You should keep in mind that most people who are in jail are very sorry for what they have done—as long as they are in jail. But for many, if not most, that repentance is relatively short-lived. As soon as someone helps to get them out of prison early, they tend to not be so sorry anymore and revert back to the behavior that got them there in the first place. The key questions to ask yourself are whether getting your daughter out on bail will help her to change and if putting a mortgage on your home would be a greater burden on you and the family than you should be required to bear under these circumstances. The Spirit will help you in your decision.

CHAPTER 16

LOANING MONEY

Knowing when or if to loan or give money to adult children is a difficult challenge for many parents. There is an underlying principle that should be taken into account whenever parents are approached by adult children for money (or any other resource, for that matter). It is the stewardship principle. In a real sense, that money is not the parents' to give. It belongs to the Lord, and they are just stewards over it (see, for example, D&C 104:54–56). While they have the right to choose how it will be used, they cannot abrogate their responsibility to use those resources in ways which will further His work on this earth—to *truly* bless His children. All decisions concerning allocation of resources should be made with this understanding in mind. In the light of this stewardship accountability, there are some general guidelines parents can follow as they determine what, if anything, they should be willing to give or loan their children.

WHEN NOT TO LOAN OR GIVE MONEY TO ADULT CHILDREN

Parents generally *should not* loan or give money when any of the following conditions exist.

The money will primarily be used to keep the child from experiencing the consequences of bad decisions. Rob and Pam Perkins had struggled with their daughter, Judy, for twenty years. When she was fifteen she began breaking the law, using drugs, and behaving immorally and irresponsibly. The Perkinses spent thousands of dollars getting her out of one jam after another. Each time they helped her, it appeared she was improving her behavior, and Rob and Pam wanted to be there for her and show their support. But it was usually only a show, or, at best, a short-lived improvement. Now Judy was in real trouble. She had defrauded her employer and was faced with a stiff jail sentence if she couldn't come up with the $5,000 she had stolen. She approached her parents for a "loan." Rob and Pam knew that it was not likely they would ever be paid back (she had never paid them back before) and didn't know what they should do.

During several previous months, Judy seemed to have made some positive progress. She was going to church, and her nonmember husband was interested in the Church as well. His background was similar to Judy's, but they both were assuming more responsibility than they had in the past. There were still some disturbing patterns that the Perkinses observed, however, that caused them to doubt that Judy had fully turned her life around. They were concerned that if they bailed her out again now, her pattern of inconsistency and self-defeating behavior would continue. On the other hand, if they didn't pay her obligation, she would spend some months in jail, and her small amount of progress might be stopped.

After much contemplation and prayer, Rob and Pam told Judy that they loved her, but this time they would not give her the money. They said that since she committed the crime, she would have to pay the consequences. She was crestfallen, but did not get angry with her parents as she had done in the past. The Perkinses felt that they had made the right decision and that this experience might be the one that would finally bring Judy to a productive, meaningful life.

This was not the end, though. Judy came back with another proposal. She told Rob and Pam that she and her husband had carefully looked at their budget and that they would be able to pay Rob and Pam back at the rate of $500 a month for ten months, if they would loan Judy the $5,000. Judy was even willing to draw up a loan agreement and sign it. Rob and Pam remained firm in their decision. They suggested to Judy that she go to her employer and make the same proposal—to pay him back at the rate of $500 a month and include generous interest. Judy replied, "But what if I miss a payment?"

"And what if you missed a payment to us?" Rob responded. She didn't say anything—just smiled sheepishly. That was the end of the conversation. Judy did go to her employer and make the proposal, handing him a check for $500 plus interest to show her good faith. He accepted the offer, and Judy paid off her debt without missing a payment. Judy faced the consequences of her actions and learned from them.

Throughout this book, we have talked much about the mistake of keeping our adult children from experiencing the consequences of their decisions. It is never easy, and there are, of course, exceptions to this rule. But that is what they are—exceptions. In most cases, parents are at least postponing any substantial progress of their adult children when they continually bail them out of difficulties the children have brought upon themselves. Debts arising from bad business decisions, credit overextension, and criminal activity are just some of the areas that fall into this category. Such bailouts rarely stop the behavior that got the adult child into his or her predicament in the first place and usually create more strain in the relationship between child and parent than would have existed if the money had not been forthcoming.

The parents will be hurt significantly if the money is not paid back. Parents are often torn between wanting to help their children and putting their own financial future at risk, as in this next real-life story. Andrew and Penny were approached by their son, Dave, for a very sizable loan. Dave was in partnership with another man in a small business, and Dave wanted to buy the other man out, but didn't have the capital to do it. His business had been doing well, and he was offering to pay Andrew and Penny a higher-than-market rate of interest on their loan. Andrew and Penny wanted to help Dave out but were concerned about losing their money. They had not been able to save much toward retirement, which they would begin within a couple of years, and they would need this money to make their retirement comfortable.

After some discussion, they decided to loan Dave the money. For the first two years, they received payments for principal and interest every month. But then Dave's business began failing, and finally he went out of business altogether. His payments became more sporadic, but Andrew and Penny were concerned about his being able to pay his personal bills and provide for the needs of his wife and small children, so they told him to just do the best he could and they would get by.

Dave felt bad when he missed payments, but he knew there was nothing else he could do. Over time, Dave got back on his feet and was able to pay his debt off completely, though it took several years more than he had planned. Andrew and Penny were glad to get it back and were not significantly compromised by having the payment of the loan drag out longer than was agreed upon.

Andrew and Penny realized they were lucky. Some of their friends hadn't done so well in loaning money to their children. They thought about what their lifestyle would have been like if they had not been paid back. They would have had to drastically curtail some of their plans and would have lived close to a subsistent life. If they had it to do over again, they probably would not have loaned Dave the money. As it turned out, Dave would have been better off too if he hadn't borrowed the money to pay off his partner.

Parents should not loan more money than they can afford to lose. Their retirement should not be put into jeopardy, and their present standard of living or financial well-being should not be compromised if there is not a payback of their loan. This is a cardinal rule. Only the most unusual circumstances should warrant consideration of an exception.

The money is being used to "buy" a better relationship with the adult child. The folly of this logic should be obvious. No acceptable relationship can ever be established on the basis of anything other than mutual respect and love. Money is not only not a substitute; its use for this purpose is a statement that neither mutual respect nor love exists in a sufficient quantity to allow any meaningful, long-lasting relationship to even be formed. If parental time and attention to an estranged adult child has not worked to improve relationships, parents should be patient and let time work in their favor. It will. Money won't.

The adult child has other acceptable options. Parents need to let their adult children learn independence by encouraging them to utilize potential resources other than their parents. Mack and his wife, Sue, were buying their first home. They qualified for a loan, but were concerned they might not be able to come up with the 10 percent down by the time escrow closed in three months. Mack was hard-working, had a good job, and was reliable. They approached Sue's father to see if he would loan them half of their down payment. This would relieve some pressure on them and also allow them to buy some furnishings for their new home. Sue's father told them that he would lend them the money that was needed to pay the down payment after they had done everything they could do to come up with the money. Mack and Sue were a little disappointed that he had not committed to a certain amount, but were grateful they would be able to move into the home. Over the next three months they pinched their pennies, and Mack did additional work on the side to earn more money. When escrow closed, they had saved enough for their down payment and even had some left over to start furnishing their home. They were glad that Sue's father had not jumped in with the money when they had asked. They both knew it would have been unlikely that they would have worked so hard to save their own money, and they would have incurred unnecessary additional debt as a result.

The natural tendency for most parents is to want to help their adult children. Giving or loaning money is one of the ways they can do this. Often, however, this act is counterproductive. Whenever such a gift or loan will tend to keep errant adult children from changing in positive ways or will put parents at financial risk, it should not be done. Money should not be given for the purpose of improving parent-child relationships or when there are better alternatives available to the adult child. Otherwise, substantial long-term harm may actually be done to the child.

DECIDING TO LOAN OR GIVE MONEY TO ADULT CHILDREN

Parents should consider loaning or giving money to their adult children when none of the above conditions exist *and* when the money would likely improve their children's spiritual, emotional, mental, or physical well-being. In making such a decision, parents should consider the potential ramifications for other members of the family—remember, what parents give to one child they may not be able to give to another. They also need to take into account the stewardship responsibility they have to recognize these resources as belonging to the Lord.

If parents decide to loan an adult child money rather than to give it to him or her, they need to clearly state that and establish a specific payback schedule and interest rate. A contract needs to be drawn up and signed by all parties concerned so there is no misunderstanding about the agreement and parental expectations. If parents are unsure whether to loan money or to give it as a gift, they are better off loaning the money. They can forgive the debt if they want to.

Whether parents give money to their adult children or loan it to them, they have a right to be involved in the children's decisions relative to the use of that money. The more of the parents' money that is involved, the more parents' input can be in those ultimate decisions.

Unwise lending or giving of money to adult children is one of the biggest causes of problems in parent–adult children relationships. In most instances, those challenges can be avoided by parents saying no when they should say no. On the other hand, parents can also be of significant help to their children with gifts or loaning of money. Determining when this should be done is not always easy. As parents seek inspiration and strive to handle the Lord's possessions as He would if He were here, they are likely to consistently make those decisions that will bless their children.

QUESTIONS & ANSWERS

Q Our son borrowed a lot of money from us. In fact, we put a second mortgage on the house to lend it to him. He has not paid any of it back, and we can't keep up the payments on that mortgage and may lose our home if he doesn't pay us. We have a signed contract with him and are thinking of suing him. What do you think we should do?

A Suing your son is a drastic step and probably would permanently damage your relationship with him, his wife, and their children (your grandchildren). Furthermore, if he hasn't paid you anything yet, it is unlikely that he would have that much you could get even if your suit was successful. If you have not already done so, see if you can work with him to pay whatever he can, whenever he can. Talk to him and his wife together about this and ask them for suggestions about solving this problem. It may be that there is nothing they can do. In that case, you will have to do the best you can on your own or with help from other members of your family. We suggest strongly, though, that you don't let this destroy your present and future relationships with him and his family. Don't lend him any more money, though!

Q My twenty-one-year-old returned missionary wants me to cosign for him so he can have a credit card. He's served a good mission and has been responsible in the past, but I'm concerned about what he might do with a credit card. Am I being unreasonable if I tell him I won't cosign?

A No, you aren't. When a parent cosigns on a credit card, he or she is literally loaning the child up to the credit limit on the card, without any say in how it will be spent. What's more, the interest rates on unpaid credit card bills are exorbitant, and the parent is on the hook for that as well. That's neither reasonable nor responsible. If your son is in school, it is likely he can qualify for a low-credit-limit card on his own. If he decides to get one, it would be well to teach him to use it only for convenience and not to borrow on it. In any case, there is not a lot of damage he can do with the low credit limit.

Q Our daughter and her husband have asked us for money for a down payment on a house, but they won't ever sit down with us to discuss the terms of a loan. I think they just think we ought to give it to them. We have told them we are willing to work something out but that we need to talk about an agreement with them. How long should we insist on getting together and drawing up something formal before we give in?

A You need to make up your minds whether this is going to be a loan or a gift. If it's a gift, let it be a gift. If it is a loan, tell them that it will be a loan, they will be required to pay the loan back as per agreement, and there will be a written contract. Tell them you will proceed no further until they sit down with you to work out the details. Let the ball be in their court then, and don't worry about it. If they want the money, they will meet with you.

Q We lent our son the money to buy a car. We have a written agreement with him, and the car is collateral to the loan. He has not made a payment to us in five months. Should we repossess the car?

A It depends on what is more important to you right now—your money or maintaining a reasonable relationship with your son. If your son has a history of flaking out on responsibilities and you have given him every chance to take care of this obligation (including adjusting payments to a more affordable level), then you may want to consider repossession. Keep in mind that such an act may do real damage to your short-term and even long-term relations with him. It still may be the best thing to do, however. If your son wants to pay you, but can't, you should be more patient. Perhaps there is some way he can work off the debt if he doesn't have the money. Be very careful on this one.

Q My son-in-law is doing freelance artwork at home and needs an expensive computer to be competitive. He is very good and conscientious, but he doesn't have the money to buy one yet and has asked me if I would help him. I like the idea of his being independent and am impressed with his initiative, but that's a lot of money. I can afford to lend it to him, but it would hurt if he couldn't pay it back. What should I do?

A If there is no other feasible source for him to get his computer and if you would not be seriously jeopardized if he couldn't pay you back, you should consider lending him the money. Be sure to set the terms of the loan so that he can reasonably make payments while he is getting started. Have a contract drawn up and signed so that he understands that this is strictly a business deal.

Q Our son borrowed a substantial amount of money from us toward a down payment on his new home. He promised to pay the loan back within one year. He got into his home and then lost his job. He got a new one, but he is not making as much money as he was making before and hasn't been able to pay off his loan to us. Do you think we should just forgive the debt?

A Whenever parents loan money, they need to consider the possibility of not being repaid and that it will ultimately be a gift to their child. You may want to wait a while before you tell him he doesn't have to repay the debt. In the meantime, you should assure him that you will be patient in the repayment of his debt so that he is not unduly worried about it. Helping our children buy homes is certainly a good use of our funds if we can afford it.

CHAPTER 17

ISSUES OF ABUSE

One of the most difficult challenges parents can have comes when they detect abuse in the home of an adult child. Whether it is spouse abuse or child abuse, parents of the adult child involved are caught in a seemingly no-win position. To do "something" to stop it is likely to alienate the adult child (or his or her spouse) and may even bring to that adult child (and perhaps to the parents of the adult child) severe consequences. On the other hand, not doing anything will almost always postpone significant, positive change from taking place in the life of the abuser, causing extensive and maybe irreparable harm to the one(s) being abused. Most importantly, needed treatment will not be forthcoming in a timely manner to aid the victim.

We believe that whether parents should do something when they know about an abusive situation in the home of an adult child must *never* be the question. Something should *always* be done!

DETERMINING IF AN ABUSIVE SITUATION EXISTS

In most instances, it is obvious if abuse exists. Either parents are eyewitnesses to it in the home of an adult child, or victims of the abuse have told them (or others) that it is occurring.

Sometimes, however, it is not so clear that an abusive situation exists. Be careful! Parents need to be *reasonably* certain that an abusive situation exists before they take significant action, because of the potentially severe consequences that may occur when such action is taken. We are aware of a woman who reported her husband's brother and his wife to their bishop and to the county social service department for alleged child abuse. This family's life was virtually put on hold while Family Services investigated the claim. Teachers at school and neighbors were interviewed, along with the parents and the children who were the alleged victims. The conclusion by all was that no abuse had taken place. In fact, the parents were not only exonerated but were considered to be model parents in many ways. Unfortunately, though, the damage was done. The family became the subject of unwarranted gossip, and the shock of it traumatized both parents and children for months. As might be expected, it destroyed the relationship between the two families—maybe permanently.

What had actually happened? The woman spoke to one of her in-laws' children after he had been given a spanking. The child apparently also said that he was being yelled at. He may or may not have embellished the incident, but he was certainly upset at the time. What the woman did not take into account was that the mother and father had been on edge because of a serious illness the mother was suffering and the subsequent financial pressures that were put on the family as they tried to keep up with expensive medical bills. The woman read something into the incident and let her imagination take it from there. In actuality, the child had an excellent ongoing relationship with his mother and father and never dreamed that what he was saying would be misconstrued. The woman jumped to the wrong conclusions and did not take time to verify them.

If there are "signs" that abuse is taking place but there is uncertainty as to what is happening, parents should carefully follow the procedures outlined in the first chapter of this section to determine if a problem exists, as well as the extent to which it exists. The consequences of doing the *wrong* thing in a nonabusive situation can be nearly as severe as the consequences of not doing the *right* thing in an abusive one.

FORMS OF ABUSE

Abuse can be defined as any action that is either intended to or in fact does demean or harm another individual. Usually, but certainly not always, abuse is perpetrated by individuals who are attempting to demonstrate their own superiority by controlling another. The abusive actions of such an individual are often manifestations of his or her own uncontrolled internal fight with feelings of gross inadequacy and are likely to be exhibited in a number of ways. The severity of his or her abusive action is measured both by how frequently it occurs and its acuteness.

Here are some common forms abusive behavior can take:

Physical abuse. This includes non-life-threatening acts such as pushing, shoving, biting, hair-pulling, slapping, pinching, and inordinate spanking, as well as brutal, even life-threatening acts that range from hitting, slugging, or shaking violently to kicking or beating with fists or objects. Physical abuse also occurs when one deprives another of essential nourishment, clothing, shelter, comfort, or sleep, as well as when one is forced to maintain painful positions for long periods of time or is unreasonably restricted in his or her movement.

Sexual abuse. Spousal abuse occurs when a husband or wife forces himself or herself sexually on his or her mate. It also takes place if a mate is compelled against his or her will to view sexually explicit pictures, videos, or movies; listen to sexually explicit audio tapes and programs; or be subjected to crude jokes or language. A child is sexually abused when he or she is involved in any sexual act with an adult or where there is inappropriate touching of his or her private parts by any adult or when the child is asked to touch the private parts of an adult. Sexual abuse also occurs when a child is shown pornography, spoken to with lewdness, or made to witness any sexual activity.

Nonphysical abuse. More frequent than physical or sexual abuse, but potentially no less demeaning, is verbal and nonverbal abuse. Verbal abuse includes yelling at, swearing at, belittling, berating, mocking, nagging, or condemning either spouse or children. Nonverbal abuse is manifested through looks, expressions, actions, and forced silence that ridicule or show disdain and contempt.

Neglect. This form of abuse is, perhaps, more subtle than the others. It results when parents will not carry out the parental responsibilities that are necessary to maintain the safety and well-being of their children. Abuse from neglect occurs when needed medical assistance is withheld, when children are subjected to unsanitary or unsafe conditions, when children are not properly nourished (physically, mentally, emotionally, and spiritually), when children are not adequately clothed or cleansed, and when children are not protected from potentially damaging influences or circumstances.

Hardly ever does an abuser restrict himself or herself to just one or two forms of abuse. Typically, abusive patterns involve many, if not all, of the forms described above. While reasons for abuse vary, in most instances chronic abuse stems from deep-seated, ongoing challenges that the abuser is inadequately dealing with. Often extensive spiritual and professional counseling is necessary if these patterns are ever to be broken.

ABUSED AND ABUSERS

Any member of a family can be a victim of abuse. Most often, however, it is either the wife or children or both who are the victims. Almost by definition, an abuser "picks" on those who are least able (or least willing) to defend themselves. That usually means that the abuser is physically bigger or stronger than his or her victim, but not always. For example, some wives abuse their husbands. While sometimes such abuse is physical (and even sexual), more often this abuse is nonphysical. Nevertheless, it is degrading and as potentially devastating as if it were physical. (We know of a man who said of the constant verbal abuse heaped upon him by his wife, "I'm not henpecked, I'm buzzard-beaked!")

It is possible for either fathers or mothers or both to be abusive to their children and stepchildren. Much of the time, the abuser has been the victim of abuse at some time in his or her life as well.

GETTING HELP WHEN ABUSE EXISTS

While parents of adult children who are being abusive or are abused can, and usually should, play a key role in trying to rectify such a situation, assistance outside the family is available and usually necessary. In most instances, outside help needs to be used if positive, permanent change is to take place. Concerned parents and grandparents are often too close to the situation to be objective. Furthermore, they do not have the training or experience to deal with chronic or severe abuse patterns. They can provide spiritual and moral encouragement, however, and in some instances may need to bring their children or grandchildren who are being abused into their home. In some states, parents *may also be required by law* to report known or suspected child abuse to government authorities.

When spouse or child abuse is suspected, the Church is usually the best place to turn to for help. For anything but minor abusive incidents, concerned parents should either make certain that their offending or offended adult child contact his or her bishop or stake president, or they should make that contact if their adult child will not. While abusive tendencies may exist as a result of any number of factors, including environmental, mental, emotional, and physical challenges, it will be through the Atonement of the Savior and following His teachings that such challenges can eventually be overcome. The bishop and stake president hold keys that will help unlock the full blessings and power of the Atonement. Furthermore, it is unlikely that complete healing can ever take place in victims of abuse without the Atonement's saving balm. Priesthood leaders, Relief Society presidents, as well as home teachers, visiting teachers, and other auxiliary leaders and teachers may prove invaluable in helping both the abused and the abuser.

The bishop or stake president can give substantial assistance not only from a spiritual standpoint, but in furnishing direction and counsel concerning other resources and legal requirements. Priesthood leaders have access to a special team at Church headquarters who provide legal and practical counsel to those leaders as they seek to help both the abuser and the victims. In addition, through LDS Family Services, needed professional counseling and foster-home placement can be provided or referred.

POSSIBLE RAMIFICATIONS OF REPORTING ABUSE

It is safe to say that once an abusive situation is brought out into the open, all who are rightfully involved outside of the immediate family will be seeking to rectify the condition. The status quo will not be allowed to continue. Obviously, the degree and consequences of such involvement will depend on the severity of the abuse and the individual circumstances that are unique to each situation. In the case of physical abuse (including sexual abuse), the law should be brought in. Some of the possible ramifications are listed below.

Professional counselors. In most states, professional counselors are required by law to report to the local government any physical or sexual abuse of minors that they become aware of through their counseling or otherwise.

The law. Whenever the state becomes involved, at the very least there will be an investigation of the alleged abusive situation. Family members, friends, and neighbors will likely be interviewed and the home inspected. Results vary widely according to the circumstance but could involve any or all of the following:

- Mandated counseling.
- Removal of the accused abuser or victims from the home.
- Ongoing monitoring by the governing social agency.
- Criminal prosecution of alleged abusers, with possible jail time resulting.

The family. The immediate family, and possibly the extended family, may undergo substantial initial and ongoing disruption not limited to the following:

- The abusing spouse or the abused spouse may be required to leave the home.
- Children may be placed in temporary or permanent foster homes, which may or may not be homes of extended family members.
- Adult children may alienate themselves from their reporting parents.
- A divorce may occur.

GRANDPARENTS AS PARENTS

If abused children need to be placed in another home, is the best alternative the home of the grandparents? Maybe and maybe not. Two key questions need to be answered before such a decision is made.

Will the children be better off with the grandparents? Some things that need to be considered here are potential age-gap identity problems, current relationships between children and grandparents, accessibility of the abusing parent to his or her children (it may or may not be desirable), and the grandparents' ability to *reasonably* provide for the children's economic, emotional, spiritual, and physical needs.

Are the grandparents willing to become parents of young children again? This is a very difficult decision. Some things to consider include the effect such a decision will have on short- and long-term plans (including retirement); the physical, mental, and emotional states of both grandparents; the degree to which established, important daily routines will be affected; and the potential change in relationships between the grandparents and their friends and other family members.

While it is usually the state that makes the ultimate determination, social workers and the courts tend to favor placing abused children in the homes of the nearest relatives, if that is a viable alternative. There are many tens of thousands of grandparents who are "doing it all over again." Is this an obligation of grandparents? Not necessarily. It is an *opportunity* to affect in powerful, positive ways one's posterity—and that for generations to come. But it is never "requisite that [we] should run faster than [we have] strength" (see Mosiah 4:27). Grandparents faced with this choice should consider all of the parenting principles discussed in this book when making such an impacting decision.

The rule for parents of adult children who are aware of abuse in the home of any of their children is the same as the rule given to the priesthood leaders of the Church: *Do not let it continue.* Regardless of the ramifications (and sometimes they will be severe), the status quo of abuse must stop. The first responsibility of parents who know of abusive situations in the home of an adult child is to protect the victims. This is their moral and legal duty. Their second responsibility is to help the perpetrator overcome his or her problem. Through relying on the Spirit, through love, and through bringing in inspired priesthood leaders who hold the sacred keys that can open the door to healing, parents will bless their children and grandchildren who are caught in the web of abuse.

QUESTIONS & ANSWERS

Q Our daughter gave birth to her son out of wedlock and has insisted on keeping the baby. That was two years ago. She refuses to let us take the child—I think because of the welfare benefits she is getting, and she refuses to change her behavior. She doesn't have a place to live permanently, but keeps moving around. I am really concerned about the baby's welfare. One of her friends told me that she has seen her give the baby beer to drink in his bottle. My husband and I have gone over to where she lives and have found our grandson outside with no one else around. He is always dirty when we see him. Our daughter is not active in the Church, and I'm sure she would not listen to a bishop. We're thinking about going over and taking the baby and bringing him home with us and letting our daughter do whatever she thinks she can do about it. What do you advise?

A You need to protect the baby, but you also need to stay within the law. If you take the baby without your daughter's permission, she could press kidnapping charges against you. If you feel there is no other alternative, you should call the child welfare department of your county Family Services and explain the situation. If you feel the baby is in imminent danger, tell them that you think the baby needs to be removed immediately. They may, on your word, send the police over to pick up the baby and place him under the care of the county until the court decides what to do. Be prepared for a long and agonizing process, but know that you are doing the right thing. You may want to consider hiring an attorney as well.

Q My wife and I do not like the way our son and his wife treat their children. Our grandchildren get hollered at and spanked a lot. We think that is damaging the children. What can we do about it?

A Directly, probably not much. It is unlikely that what they are doing constitutes legal abuse. What you can do is to try to teach and exemplify the Savior in all that you do with them. Holding a joint family night with them where principles that are outlined in Doctrine and Covenants 121:41–46 are discussed may be effective. Be careful not to undermine the parental authority of your children, but also be aware of actions that may, in fact, be injurious to the safety and well-being of your grandchildren. The Spirit will guide you.

Q Our son and daughter-in-law had their first baby (a boy) about six months ago. The baby cries a lot, and our daughter-in-law yells at him all the time. We have even seen her shake him. We have commented about the situation to our son, but he just shakes his head and shrugs his shoulders. Is this just a matter between the two of them, or should we do something? We don't think our daughter-in-law would ever purposely do anything to hurt her baby, but she might accidentally when she gets so frustrated.

A It may be that your daughter-in-law needs professional counseling. You should talk to your son about the potential harm (both physical and emotional) that your daughter-in-law's actions pose to their son and suggest that he talk to his wife about getting some help. If he won't do anything about it and you are genuinely concerned about the baby being harmed, you should talk directly to their bishop. Be prepared for some possible alienation between you and your son and his wife.

Q Our daughter has been divorced twice. She has an apartment nearby and lives there with her three children. While we don't think the children are in any immediate danger, she does leave them alone a lot. She doesn't have a regular job and lives off welfare. She has guys sleep over all of the time, and we know she uses drugs (although she is not an addict). How can we get the children out of such a bad environment?

A Not easily. If there appears to be "reasonable" stability in the home, even under the conditions you have described, it is not likely that the law will remove the children. Unless you have reason to believe there is real danger there, you probably don't want to try that. A failed attempt will not only keep the children where they are, but will probably alienate your daughter, and she may keep you from having any contact with her children at all. Offer to have the children over to your home as much as possible.

You may even want to tell her that you are willing to have the children live with you for a while until she gets herself settled and gets a good job. Keep your eyes open, and if you see serious neglect that places the children in harm's way, be prepared to bring in the law.

Q My daughter has been married for three years. She and her husband were married in the temple and have a baby. He has a vile temper and has been "physical" with her. She says that he just "pushes" her sometimes, but I have seen bruises on her arms, and when I ask her where she got them, she tells me she bumped into the dresser or the doorway. When I ask if her husband has hit her, she says, "Not really," and drops the conversation. They are both active in the Church. What can I do when my daughter won't admit that she is being abused?

A Talk to their bishop. Explain your concerns and let him take it from there. You may want to ask the bishop to keep your conversation confidential. If your son-in-law is abusing your daughter (and it sounds like he is), he is breaking the law, and the law may ultimately need to be involved. Without question, he needs help, and your daughter needs to be protected and may need counseling as well.

Q We are considering contacting county Family Services to report the squalid conditions our two little grandchildren live in. Their father (our son) and their mother (our son's live-in girlfriend) are always partying, and the children are surrounded by their drug-using, immoral friends. We are pretty sure the county will take the children out of the home. If they do, will they give us custody? We want it!

A It depends. If at all possible, the courts usually like to place abused children in the home of people they know and love. They will do what they think will be best for the children, however. A lot depends on the recommendations of the county social worker assigned to the case. You will be interviewed and your home inspected for possible placement. Just because you are willing to take them doesn't mean that it will happen. If you are concerned that you may not get them placed with you, you might want to consider hiring an attorney to represent your interests.

Q Our grandson (he's five) is currently in a state-mandated foster home while the courts are considering his permanent placement. Our daughter (his mother) is in jail and will probably be there for several years. Nobody knows where his father is. The county social worker who has been assigned to our grandson's case has asked us if we would take legal custody of him if it was offered. We would like to, but my husband and I are both in our late sixties. He is in failing health, and I don't know that I am up to raising a child at my age. We are living on social security and don't really have anything extra to pay for the additional costs that come with raising a child. We have no other family members that he could live with. We love our grandson and want to do what is best for him. What should we do?

A The well-being of your grandson needs to be your first concern. Your choice should be made after consulting with your bishop and seeking the Spirit for guidance. If, because of your situation (age, health, and income), you do not feel you can adequately care for him, that is not something you should feel guilty about. However, you should counsel with your bishop and LDS Family Services to determine possible LDS foster homes that you could recommend to the court for consideration, and you should seek to have regular contact with him after he is placed.

Q A year ago our daughter, who was divorced, remarried a man who was also divorced. They are both very active in the Church. She brought her daughter, who is now eight, into that marriage, and her current husband has two sons, but they live with his former wife. A few months ago my granddaughter told me that her "new daddy" keeps "tickling" her, and sometimes it hurts. When I asked her where he tickled her, she pointed to her private parts. I told my daughter about the conversation, and she shrugged it off. She got upset with me for thinking it may not have been innocent. The other day I asked my granddaughter if her daddy was still tickling her. She said that he had stopped for a while, but was now doing it again, and she didn't like it. She said that he was tickling her in the same place both outside and underneath her clothing. I am reluctant to go back to my daughter because of her first response. What do you think I should do?

A Go back to your daughter and tell her your concerns. Ask that the two of you meet with your granddaughter and have her tell her mother what she has told you. If your granddaughter confirms her story, your daughter should then confront her husband. If he admits to it, they should both set an appointment to meet with their bishop for counsel and direction. If he does not admit to it, your daughter should meet with the bishop on her own for counsel and direction. If your daughter refuses to go to her bishop and you feel *reasonably* certain that sexual molestation is taking place, then you go to your bishop or stake president. He will give you direction about your legal obligation and will take it from there. Remember that you have a responsibility to protect your granddaughter which takes precedence over every other consideration. Be aware that your daughter and her husband may become alienated from you and that the law will likely become involved.

Q My daughter has confided in me that her husband insists that she watch pornographic videos with him before they make love and that she perform sexual acts that she feels very uncomfortable with. She has told him she does not want to do this, but he tells her he needs this and in a marriage relationship "anything goes." She does not want to offend him so keeps quiet about it, but I can see it is really getting to her. What should I suggest?

A Your daughter needs to see her bishop. Virtue is virtue and applies equally within a marriage and outside of a marriage. No spouse has the right to impose upon his or her mate practices that are offensive, carnal, or lust-generated. It is likely that unless your son-in-law and daughter receive some spiritual (and maybe professional) counsel, both their spiritual well-being and their marriage may ultimately be threatened.

CHAPTER 18

ESTRANGED ADULT CHILDREN

Virtually all of the challenges with adult children that are discussed in this section of the book can bring about alienation of adult children from their parents. In addition, parents or their adult children may be untactful, insensitive, careless, or downright mean in their conversations and dealings with each other. Even in good relationships, misunderstandings naturally occur as imperfect people deal with imperfect people. Sometimes this parent–adult child estrangement is short-lived, but often it is prolonged, even lasting for the rest of the parents' lives.

STEPS TOWARD OVERCOMING ESTRANGEMENT

Can parents do anything to bring down barriers of resentment and hostility when such situations exist? They can try! While nothing is guaranteed, the very *attempt* by parents to reestablish good relations with their children sends the unmistakable message that the parents *care*. Sooner or later, that message will likely get through. Here are some principles that may be helpful in this attempt.

Be willing to say, "I'm sorry." Pride usually gets in the way of any potential reconciliation. Swallow it! Take a long, objective look at what you did or did not do that has *at least* exacerbated the present estrangement between you and your adult child. Then admit your weakness and mistakes and apologize. "I am sorry" are magic words. They do not connote weakness; they indicate love and a desire to do things better. In apologizing, you also need to be specific about what you are apologizing for so there will not be further misunderstanding. For example, you should not apologize to an adult child who has been violating the standards of your home for removing him from your house. It would be appropriate, however, to express sorrow that he or she is no longer with you and apologize for any anger or resentment that you have demonstrated toward him or her in this process.

Be willing to forgive. If you have been offended by one of your adult children, put it behind you. The Lord will forgive whomever He wants to, but we are required to forgive everyone, and virtually all of the time (see D&C 64:9–11). You can be certain that no significant reconciliation will ever come about until parents are willing to forgive their children who have offended them, *even if those children have not repented or asked for forgiveness.* If parents are *willing* to forgive, they will be aided in that process by the grace of Christ, who has promised this grace in sufficiency to all who will see their own weakness and humble themselves before Him (see Ether 12:27).

Do not compromise standards and beliefs for the sake of improving relationships. Is full reconciliation with our adult children worth *any* price? No, it is not. If the price is that we tacitly or actively sustain that child in his or her behavior that is self-destructive or detrimental to the well-being of others, it is too high. Good parents will always strive to do that which is *best* for their adult children. To establish better relationships is never a justification for violating this cardinal rule of parenting. Paradoxically, parents who are unflinching in their righteous expectations of their adult children are most likely to ultimately establish the kind of relationships they desire. Why? Because their children will come to know that their parents love them and are doing what is best for them.

Keep trying. Time is on the side of parents who don't quit in their attempts to reach their children. Kindness, compassion, and patience are key ingredients in this process. Remember that while it is important that parents never give up, it is also critical that they not become so absorbed in this objective that it dominates their lives. To do so is tantamount to turning one's happiness and peace over to another, and that should never be done. Balance and judgment are also requisites to establishing acceptable relationships with children.

MAKING CONTACT

How do you get through to children who will not respond to your overtures? There is no one solution here. And when children ignore parents' attempts to contact them, frustration easily sets in. But if parents know where their alienated children are, there are some simple things that they can do to at least keep their adult child aware of their desires to make contact.

Write regularly. As long as your letters (or e-mail messages) are not being returned with the message, "No such person at this address," keep writing. There are many instances where children ultimately respond after a long period of refusing to even open letters they received from their parents. Some children who have finally been reconciled to their parents after ignoring their communication efforts later testify that they could not understand why their parents continued so faithfully to try to make contact, but that this showed their parents loved them. We know of some parents who send post-cards so the message can be read on the way from the mailbox or by other members of the family without their having to open anything.

Leave messages on answering machines. These should be left regularly, but need to be brief and innocuous. The child will at least know that his or her parent is trying, and that is likely to eventually help soften his or her heart.

Contact your child's priesthood leaders. Contact the bishop in the area where your estranged child lives and let him help you make contact and mend fences. While alienated adult children may not be active in the Church, they will not have forgotten their positive experiences with the Church when they were younger, and they are likely to at least receive Church leaders with cordiality. They may even respond to an inspired priesthood leader's efforts.

Pray for them. Pray for them every day. Put their names on the temple prayer rolls and remind other members of your family to include them in their prayers. There is power in prayer. You will receive comfort and assurances as a result, and the force of your pleading may touch their hearts and bring them back.

RESTARTING COMMUNICATION

When alienation between parent and an adult child has existed for a long period of time but circumstances have now allowed for some communication to take place, there is often an uncertainty as to when to start up that communication or what to say. By definition the relationship is fragile, and it is only natural for parents to be concerned about saying or doing something that will damage it again. Here are some suggestions in restarting communications with alienated children:

Follow the Spirit. This is key. When the Spirit is sought, it is likely that the words that are used will be the "right" ones or at least understood by the adult child in the right way.

Start from where you are. The focus needs to be on the present and the future. Parents need to do their best to begin *today* to build a relationship as of *today,* without worrying too much about what has taken place in the past. Insisting on knowing all that has gone on in an adult child's life while he or she was estranged from you is usually a negative approach and a one-way ticket back to alienation.

Get together as quickly as possible. Communication is more likely to be what you want it to be if it is face-to-face. Neutral activities at neutral places are a good way to begin. Good food and memorable places will add warmth. Usually the parents will need to lead out, both in making the appointment and generating conversation. Parents need to be flexible and accommodating in their schedules to meet with their children's time constraints.

Make it easy for the adult child to talk. Talk about interests of the adult child. The important thing is that communication is taking place, not what the topic is. Parents need to be satisfied that communication is now happening. Important topics can be discussed later.

Parents provide "updates" first. It is likely that parents and children who are alienated from one another haven't been aware of what has been happening in the lives of the others. Parents should lead out in providing news of events and happenings in their lives and in the lives of other family members. Then let the adult child talk, *if he or she wants to.* Sometimes these conversations are one-sided at first, but over time are likely to become balanced.

Don't rush it. Don't try to put this relationship into hyper-speed. It's tough to have to wait after you see some progress in a fragile relationship, but wise parents will let reconciliation go at its own pace. Moving too fast may cause a regression that will take much longer to resolve. It is better to appreciate every step. By expecting small improvements, you are not likely to be disappointed. If larger ones come, you can enjoy the thrill of having your expectations exceeded by the actual outcome.

Express love. An outward expression of love can do wonders. Most parties err on the side of speaking too little love rather than too much, although emotions can become a problem for some. Of course we are not speaking of maudlin outbursts, but of simple, deeply felt statements (e.g., "I have been thinking about you a lot"; "You have been in my prayers"; "I have missed you"; "I love you").

It is the parents' responsibility to do everything within their power to bring about reconciliation with their estranged children. While this does not mean they are expected either to sacrifice their own well-being or to enable an errant adult child, it does mean they are to put forth a heartfelt, concerted effort to eliminate hard feelings and bring about an ultimate and permanent reuniting of their family.

QUESTIONS & ANSWERS

Q My daughter has told me not to ever come to her house again, and if I do she will call the police. What should I do?

A Don't go. That is her home, and you need to abide by her wishes whether there is a legal threat or not. You should continue, however, to invite dialogue. This will probably be best done by letter to begin with, then short phone calls just to make sure she is okay. Avoid being combative and be willing to apologize if you have done something to offend her. Be patient. Reestablishing relationships in this kind of situation may take a long time.

Q How concerned should we be about our adult children when they don't seem to want us to be involved in their lives? They never return our calls or write us, and when we indicate we would like to come to visit them, they discourage us from doing so.

A   Continue to show interest in them, but do it casually and not so often as to "bug" them. If you do stop by to visit them, make it short. Periodic notes and phone calls are appropriate. Give it time.

Q   Our daughter married a man who was of a different ethnic culture. We didn't want her to do that and were very vocal about it right up to the time she married him. They were married in the temple and are active in the Church, but since the wedding neither one of them wants anything to do with us. It's been two years. Both my wife and I have changed our views about our son-in-law and probably shouldn't have made such a big deal of his culture in the first place. What can we do to get back on good terms with them when they refuse to have any contact with us?

A   You might try working with their bishop. Contact him and explain your situation and see if he will serve as an intermediary for you. Be willing to sincerely apologize and express love. Don't expect miracles, though. It is likely that substantial time will pass before they are convinced that you not only accept their marriage, but that you love *both* of them. You will need to bend over backwards to demonstrate this change in your hearts.

Q   My daughter is living with a man whom she has never married. She was very strong in the Church but gave it up. They have three children. They don't care about having contact with me, but if I call, she will talk. She doesn't think I should visit. They live in another part of the country, and I have never seen these three grandchildren. Do you think I should visit them?

A   You should try to get to know those kids. You can have a very powerful influence on their lives if you do, and it is possible that they may be the way your daughter is brought back into the Church and she and their father ultimately marry. Your daughter knows how you feel about what she is doing, and you don't have to keep mentioning it. What you do need to do is to continually express your love for her. For the time being, concentrate on being a grandmother, and let the marriage issue take care of itself. Tell your daughter you would love to come and visit them. You may even want to be a bit aggressive about that—not insisting, but letting her know this is something that is very important to you. If you do go, strive to be the perfect mother, grandmother, and guest. Then you might consider inviting your daughter's family (including her "live-in") to come and visit you. Take this one step at a time.

Q Our son left home when he was in his late teens and gave us nothing but trouble all through his high school years. He was constantly verbally abusive to his siblings and to us, stole money from all of us, and refused to live our standards either in our home or out of it. When he left we felt like saying, "Good riddance!" He's been gone for a couple of years now. He floats around and calls us collect from time to time (usually to ask for money, which we don't give him most of the time). We've been thinking about refusing to accept his collect phone calls. Do you think we would be wrong if we did?

A You don't need to give him money, and you don't need to bring him back into your home, but you do need to try to maintain communication. For the time being, accepting his collect phone calls seems to be the way to do that. Your conversations (at least on your end) should be upbeat and family oriented. Express your love and your concern for his well-being. Time is on your side, so don't cut him off completely.

Q I have done everything I know of to get my daughter to talk to me again, but she won't do it. I write letters and she returns them unopened. I used to call her, but now she has an unlisted phone number. I was unfaithful to my husband (her father) and left him a few years ago, and while I have taken care of everything with the Church and feel the Lord has forgiven me, my daughter will not forgive me and won't have anything to do with me. It worries me sick. I can't sleep because it is always on my mind. What do you suggest?

A You have control over what you do, not over what your daughter does. You have done and are doing all that you can and should do. Continue to do that and get on with your life (easier said than done, huh?). Keep writing the letters to your daughter, though. It is probable that some day she will read them. Keep praying that your daughter's heart will be softened, and stop beating yourself for something that the Lord has forgiven *and that your daughter should*. Be patient with her too. As she sees what is happening with you as a result of your repentance and as she grows spiritually, she will likely come around. In the meantime, try to stop worrying about that which is out of your control.

CHAPTER 19

IN-LAWS AND POTENTIAL IN-LAWS

President James E. Faust, in a stake conference that he presided at years ago as a member of the Quorum of the Twelve, announced to the congregation that his daughter and "son-in-love" were there. He went on to talk about his son-in-law's virtues that made him his son-in-*love* and expressed his gratitude for his being a part of his family.

We have had that same kind of relationship with our in-law parents. Our mothers-in-law have stayed with us and our wives at the births of our children and have spent countless hours throughout the years quietly going about darning socks and mending clothes, while our fathers-in-law have fixed things around our homes that needed attention. They have been our friends and have loved us as if we were their own children, and we have loved them.

But not all parents or children have this kind of relationship with their in-laws, and not all parents or children have this kind of in-laws! Perhaps no challenge that adult parents have with their married children is more common than strains put on the family because of in-law tensions. However, while good in-law relationships require effort from everyone involved, the consistent, patient attempt on the part of parents to make those associations as positive as possible (even if that effort is initially unilateral) will do much to ultimately establish acceptable, even meaningful, relationships.

POTENTIAL IN-LAWS

Efforts to establish affinity with in-law children are most effective when they begin even before they are in-laws. This "stitch-in-time-saves-nine" principle is critical. When an adult son or daughter is dating someone "seriously," mom and dad need to "seriously" consider that young woman or man as a potential in-law. It is during this time of courtship that parents can either welcome this potential new member of the family or alienate themselves. The effects of either decision will likely be felt for years after a marriage takes place.

So what do parents do if either one or both do not want their child to marry the one he or she is dating? Garth Hanson (one of the book's authors) told his children as they were growing up that he would "counsel" them exactly how he felt when they brought a marriage "candidate" home. He also said that if they told him they were going to marry this person even though he had counseled against it, he would back off and support their choice. Garth resisted the partner selection of three of his four children. They told him to back off, and he did. In each case his children married that person, and Garth now feels that each married the "right" one. He feels sure that his procedure was right and that each child made the proper selection. *None of his in-law children was offended in the process.*

Of course, it doesn't always work out this way. Sometimes children marry the "wrong" person, contrary to their parents' counsel. But even if this happens, no purpose is served by parents being rude or aloof to or alienated from their potential son- or daughter-in-law, regardless of how displeasing he or she may be. In fact, it is quite likely that vindictive parents will only exacerbate an already very difficult situation, setting the stage for long-term estrangement from their own children and grandchildren.

Here are some observations that should be helpful in establishing acceptable pre-in-law relationships.

- Children will *usually* follow their parents' teachings and counsel as they make marriage decisions.
- Children can follow their parents' counsel in spouse selection and still not come up with a spouse who fits parental expectations.
- Most children want to be (and need to be) independent when selecting a spouse.
- Children will *usually* make the marriage decision

that is best for them if they have been taught and
counseled well and if they are left to work out their
own decisions.

- Parents are most effective when they make themselves
available for counsel and interaction during the
marriage-decision process, but are not overbearing and
insistent.
- Parents need to be ultra-careful about what they say
between the time the decision is tentative and when it
becomes final. Negative comments can build barriers
that may be difficult to ever remove.
- Parents should actively seek to build a positive relationship with their children's potential spouse.

IN-LAW CHILDREN

There is a key principle, succinctly expressed in scripture, that
should form the basis of parental involvement with a married adult
child and his or her spouse: "For this cause shall a man *leave* his father
and mother, and cleave to his wife; and they twain shall be one flesh:
so then they are no more twain, but one flesh" (see Mark 10:7–8;
italics added). With the marriage of a child, there is a new family unit
created which is autonomous in most respects. The role of the parents
in this *new* husband-wife/father-mother *team* is to love always, and to
counsel or assist carefully and usually only when invited to do so.
Accepting your son or daughter as being inseparably connected with
his or her spouse pays the in-law spouse the highest compliment and
will open the door wide for his or her melding into your extended
family on equal footing with every other member. This usually does
not occur either immediately or automatically. Rather, it is a process
that the parents of adult children need to continually work on. Here
are some suggestions and observations.

- In-law children have not been around you for the
twenty-plus years your children have. Give them time
to get used to you, your sense of humor, your
strengths, and your weaknesses.

- Accept the fact that the "personality" of your overall family will change with the addition of each new in-law child. This change will almost always be a positive one, if parents will strive to make it so.
- Keep to yourself negative thoughts and criticisms about what your in-law child is or is not doing.
- Realize that there will likely be significant differences in the way your married children handle their money, fix their food, keep their home, and discipline their children. As long as they are surviving and not using your resources, let them be (unless, of course, there is child or spouse abuse).
- Respect decisions made by your married children. While parental counsel given *before* a decision is made may be appropriate, "I-told-you-so" comments after a decision is made are rarely justified.
- Let your married children and their spouses form their own family traditions even if they differ markedly from what you have established.
- When you visit the home of your married children, remember you are their guests, not their supervisors.
- Avoid being involved in your children's husband-wife disagreements.
- When you call on the phone, try to speak to both your child and his or her spouse.
- Invite your married children to attend *every* family function, but do not make them feel obligated to do so.
- Willingly share your child and his or her spouse with in-law parents and family at holidays and throughout the year.
- If you have said or done something to offend your child's spouse, apologize quickly. If your child's spouse has done or said something to offend you, forget it!

FAMILY OF IN-LAW CHILDREN

Sometimes the challenge parents have is not so much with their in-law children as with the parents of those in-law children. When you see your daughter-in-law's parents interface with *your* child and his spouse in ways that run counter to some or all of the observations we have made above, what do you do? And when those in-law parents are unreasonably demanding in the amount of time they expect your child and his family to spend with them, or shower on them gifts, money, and property that you do not have the means to give (or, perhaps, don't feel it is right to give), should you become upset and try to stop it somehow? Likewise, when your child and his family spend far more of their time with his in-laws than they do with you, should you insist that they be with you at least an equal amount of time?

Of course, these are not easy questions to answer. Usually, what is "best" is to just go on doing what you think is the right thing to do in your relationship with your married children and their spouses and let them work out their relationship with the in-law parents. Your counsel, suggestions, and observations regarding the "other parents" are probably best kept to yourself unless your children ask you for them. Even then, be careful what you say.

What you can do is be proactive in establishing good communications between you and your in-law child's parents and family. Sending Christmas cards, sharing important family events, and getting together socially when the occasion allows are ways to enhance that communication and establish good relationships that can help prevent potential in-law strains in the future.

PREPARING OUR CHILDREN TO BE GOOD IN-LAWS

There is something that parents can do before their children ever get married to help them make their relationship with their future in-laws as good as they can make it. Teach them how to be a good son-in-law or daughter-in-law. While this instruction is best done before a marriage, it can also be done after (perhaps with a little more tact and in a spirit of suggestion). Here are some concepts that ought to be covered:

- Treat in-law parents with respect.
- Try to visit and communicate with in-law parents frequently. Don't send your spouse alone to visit his or her parents on a regular basis; go with him or her.
- Don't call your in-law parents by their first names.
- Don't assume you can live in your in-law's home as casually as you lived in your own parents' home—especially the first few years of marriage.
- Make a concerted effort to be part of conversations with in-law parents on every visit.
- Accept without criticism or negative comment the traditions of in-law parents on birthdays, special events, and holidays.
- Eat what they prepare.
- Clean up after yourself while in their home.
- Look for ways to help in-law parents while in their home (e.g., participating in work projects, preparing meals, doing the dishes, keeping your room clean, and so on).
- Treat your spouse (their child) with respect and kindness always, but especially in their presence.
- Treat your spouse's siblings with respect.
- Work hard at creating a loving, solid relationship with your in-law parents.

QUESTIONS & ANSWERS

Q My son wants to marry a young woman who is not of our culture (we are African-American, and she is Caucasian). We are really concerned about this, even though they are planning a temple wedding. We like her, but I don't think it's going to work out. What should I do?

A It is appropriate to counsel our adult children on any condition that could provide challenges to a marriage, including different cultural, educational, or economic backgrounds. The counsel should be limited to the "here are some things that you might want to consider . . ." variety, rather than the "if you want to be happy, you'd better not . . ." kind. Encourage your son to seek the Spirit and let him make his own decision. If he chooses to marry her, embrace her as if she were your own daughter and sustain their marriage in every way possible.

Q How can you avoid irreparable harm if you resist the marriage partner selection of your children, then change to supporting them after they have made the decision to marry against your counsel?

A The secret here is the tone and timing of your counsel. The tone needs to be kind and undemanding. It is appropriate to express your strong reservations, if you have them, but you need to emphasize your confidence in your son or daughter making the right choice and your commitment to sustain that choice. Your counsel should not take on a pattern of harping and nagging; otherwise, irreparable harm may be done. The timing of your counsel is likewise important. It should come *before* the decision is made. It should stop *after* that decision.

Q I don't feel comfortable around my daughter-in-law. I feel like I am walking on eggs when we are together. I get along well with all of my sons-in-law, but I feel like I am in competition with her. What should I do?

A Realize that she may, in fact, perceive you as being a competitor. You have been the woman in your son's life up until now, and everything he sees his wife doing he is probably, at least mentally (and maybe even verbally), comparing to what he has seen you do. Unwisely, he may be talking about her cooking in relationship to yours, her housekeeping in relationship to yours, and so on. Try to build her confidence by complimenting her (make it real and sincere, though), spending meaningful one-on-one time with her (take her out to lunch or on an outing from time to time with just the two of you), and make a point of telling her in front of your son what you like about the way she is doing something. Give her time to warm up. If she doesn't change, try to get used to walking on eggs, and keep walking!

Q What would you do with a son-in-law who would rather read a
   book than go to a family reunion or family gathering?

A Try to understand him and be patient. This is not unusual, particularly for someone who is not used to attending large family
   outings. Continue to invite him and his family to your family
   functions, but don't pressure them. When they come, enjoy being
   with your daughter and your grandchildren, and let him do what
   makes him feel most comfortable. You might even consider
   having some books there for him to read. Try to spend one-on-
   one time with him at the event, and thank him for being there
   and bringing his family. Don't judge him, and give it time. He
   may never come to the point that he enjoys being with all of the
   family, but your relationship with him will not be strained.

Q My daughter-in-law doesn't like me. She has told me so. She
   won't come and visit, and she won't let her children visit either.
   What should I do?

A There is not much you can do other than be kind (not condescending) to her. You might try telling her that you are aware of
   the way she feels and that you do not want to antagonize her in
   any way, but you would like to be able to visit with your grandchildren from time to time. See if you can work out an arrangement that would be acceptable to her, but don't push her too
   hard. Continue to invite them to events. Never circumvent the
   parents and go directly to the children with those invitations,
   however. Remember that your son and daughter-in-law are in
   charge of their family, and respect that responsibility. Keep trying.

Q What do parents do when two daughters-in-law do not get along
   with each other when the family gets together? Their husbands,
   our sons, were the best of friends throughout their childhood, but
   these two girls fight all of the time when they are together.

A You may want to reduce the number of family gatherings where
   all of your family members are invited. When you do have both
   daughters-in-law at the same function, plan assignments and
   activities ahead of time to keep them separated as much as
   possible. In the meantime, try to serve as a mediator between

them without taking sides or making judgments. Spend one-on-one time with each daughter-in-law to increase your closeness to them. Their respect and love for you will likely be a tempering influence on their tendencies to flare up when the other sister-in-law is around. Time will likely bring a maturation to both of these women that will assuage, if not eliminate, their dislike for one another, so be patient.

Q I was against my daughter marrying her husband right from the beginning, and my worst fears have been realized. He has no ambition to get ahead and is satisfied to work for near minimum wages, which forces my daughter to also work in order to make ends meet. When I tell my daughter she needs to tell him to start doing something with his life, she tells me to leave them alone. I love my daughter and don't want to alienate her, but I can't just sit by and watch her lazy husband drag her down with him. What should I do?

A Abide by your daughter's request and leave them alone. We each have our own clocks, and it is possible that your son-in-law will ultimately grow out of his lethargy. Then again, maybe he won't. In either case, it is not likely that you can either speed up the process or bring about the change. If you insist on trying to create discontent in your daughter's mind, you will likely see this situation blow up in your face, and your relationship with your daughter will be the casualty. Your best bet is to strive to improve your relationship with your son-in-law and let him live his life as he wants to.

Q What can I do to help make my daughter-in-law a better mother and better wife? I really like her, but she is so immature!

A *Show* her how by the way you are living your own life, rather than trying to *make* her into your perception of what constitutes a good mother or a good wife. Avoid criticizing her or correcting her mistakes. Rather, invite her to ask you questions and come to you if she needs help with anything. Don't push yourself on her, but be available for counseling and direction if she seeks it. Remember, you were once very young too.

Q Our son is having a difficult time coping with the strange traditions of his in-laws. For example, he and his wife went over to her parents' home for Christmas Eve dinner, and all they had was oyster stew and crackers! He sat and waited for the rest of the meal to come, but that's all there was. He complained about it and offended his in-laws. He asked us what we thought he should do about it. What is your advice?

A Tell your son to apologize to his in-laws for being such a boor and then accept and cheerfully go along with the traditions of his wife's family. He does not have to adopt them into his own family, but he does need to honor them when he is with them.

Q Our son's in-laws are well-to-do and have a much nicer home than we do. The kids enjoy being at their house much more than at ours. We feel bad that we don't see them as often, but we just can't compete. What can we do?

A Don't try to compete; just do what you do best. Invite them over often, and when they come over to your home, make them comfortable, pay attention to them, prepare good meals, and have fun. There are plenty of activities that don't cost a lot of money but are at least as enjoyable as those that do. For example, family games, picnics, quilting or canning projects, storytelling, and just plain visiting. Relaxing and not worrying about it are probably the best things you can do.

Q We are really uncomfortable when the "other" grandparents are at the same events that we are, like baptisms, blessings, ordinations, and graduations. They monopolize the attention of our grandchildren and are very condescending to us. We don't like them, and they don't like us. Do you think we should just avoid going to activities that involve our grandchildren if they are going to be there? We don't want to ruin the event for our grandchildren and our son and his wife.

A Keep going. Stop reacting. While it is not necessary for you and the "other" grandparents to become best friends, it is important that you make every effort to be cordial to them. Remember that you are sharing your son with them and they are sharing their daughter with you. A continued bad relationship between the grandparents could affect their marriage and the happiness of your grandchildren. You can't do much about the unacceptable behavior of the other grandparents, but you don't need to give them "cause" for such behavior.

CHAPTER 20

WHEN AN ADULT CHILD DIVORCES

Amber and Don were deeply in love. They both came from solid LDS families, and Don was a returned missionary. They were both still in school when they married in the temple. Amber finished her junior year, then dropped out so she could earn the money necessary for Don to continue his education in medicine. She became pregnant during Don's last year of medical school. She began working part-time after the baby was born, and Don was bringing some money in through his interning.

A second baby was born a year into his residency. For the last year of his residency, their marriage was strained. Then, just a few weeks before he would finish his program and begin private practice, Don told Amber he wanted a divorce. He said he had been seeing another woman and was no longer in love with her. He packed up a few of his things and left the house.

Amber sat stunned, literally unable to move. Over the past months Don had become less and less communicative and spent more and more time away from home. Amber had credited his behavior to the strains and demands of his residency. She had never expected anything like this. After the initial shock had passed, she just sat on the floor, too overwhelmed to even cry.

"What will my friends think of me being divorced? Nobody in my family is divorced!"

"What did I do wrong? I must be a lousy wife for him to want to leave me for somebody else!"

"How can I support my children? I don't even have a college degree!"

"How could he do this to me after I put him through medical school? I'm going to get everything I can from him!"

"What can I say to the children? They won't understand that their daddy has gone!"

"Who will keep track of the bills and fix the car and mow the lawn and unplug the drain?"

"What am I going to do now? Who is going to help me?"

A hundred other questions flooded her mind through her numbness and disbelief. Finally, she picked up the phone and called her parents.

What would you say if you were her mother or father? What would you do? What would you say or do if you were Don's parents?

Like it or not, conscientious parents of adult children who are contemplating a divorce will be affected by, and involved with, what is happening with their child and his or her spouse. That involvement and change in relationships will continue if the divorce occurs and the adult child is left single, or even if he or she ultimately remarries. Unfortunately, it is becoming more and more likely that LDS parents will witness the divorce of at least one of their children.

ADULT CHILDREN ENCOUNTERING A DIVORCE

The weight of a pending or potential divorce is so onerous as to be virtually debilitating to those going through it. Virtually everything else in their lives becomes less important than dealing with this emotional and spiritual disaster. It is not only absorbing, but consuming. There is much that caring parents can do to assist their child through this gauntlet:

- Be supportive, be available, and listen, listen, listen.
- Don't judge, but patiently encourage your son or daughter to examine his or her own life to see what he or she should do to change, if anything, to avert a divorce.
- Encourage *and help* your child to try everything reasonable (and appropriate) before accepting divorce as inevitable (e.g., using professional counseling,

involving priesthood and Relief Society leaders, and getting legal advice).

- Give counsel, but don't preach or insist that your child do what you are counseling him or her to do.
- Give priesthood blessings.
- Seek guidance from the Holy Ghost.
- Encourage your son or daughter to rely on the Savior. The gospel is the way to peace. His grace is real and must be sought, and the temple and scriptures hold answers.
- Be patient with your adult child's fears, anticipate them, and do what is needed to try to alleviate them.
- Help build your son or daughter's self-confidence. It is likely shattered with this experience.
- Take one step at a time. Don't force decisions; rather, give the situation time to define itself fully. Sometimes the "answers" are not there until time passes.
- Spend extra time with the grandchildren. They are likely to be highly susceptible to feelings of insecurity and rejection.
- Encourage your son or daughter to keep busy. Depression and futility are most likely to occur when minds and bodies are not meaningfully engaged.
- Help your adult child to not become bitter and spiteful. These reactions can ultimately be more personally destructive than the divorce itself.
- Continually express your love and acceptance of your son or daughter.

WHEN DIVORCE MAY BE JUSTIFIED

Rarely is a divorce ever justified, but there are some instances when it may be the only viable answer. Even in these instances, a divorce should not be pursued without receiving appropriate counsel from Church leaders and seeking guidance from the Spirit. As you counsel with your son or daughter who may be considering a divorce, the following circumstances may be severe enough to justify such a solution.

- Your adult child or your grandchildren are subjected to chronic physical or sexual abuse by his or her spouse.
- Your child's spouse is verbally and emotionally abusive and refuses to change.
- Your son's or daughter's spouse is unfaithful and will not repent.
- Your child's husband or wife seeks to destroy the faith and testimony of your adult child or your grandchildren.
- Your son's or daughter's spouse is involved in criminal activity.
- The husband or wife of your adult child refuses to carry out his or her basic responsibilities as spouse or parent to the severe detriment of your son or daughter or your grandchildren.

WHEN ADULT CHILDREN BECOME SINGLE AGAIN

If there ever is a time when an adult child needs the support and assistance of his or her parents, it is when he or she has lost (by divorce or death) spousal commitment and companionship. The adult child is left as sole emotional, spiritual, and economic provider for himself or herself and possibly for his or her children. Parents of these adult children need to be prepared to help subsidize their now-single child in those areas where a need exists and to the extent the parents are capable or willing to do so.

Resources that parents may be called upon to provide include spiritual and temporal counseling, money, housing, food, clothing, insurance, and volunteer labor (like babysitting, home repairs, and errand running). Whether or not parents' resources *should* be used is not so much the question as *what* should be used, *how much, when,* and for *how long.* In virtually every instance, parents of adult children who are struggling in this kind of situation need to help them. Parents should:

- Be willing to do whatever is *needed* to help their child, even if sacrifice is involved.
- Assist their single adult children to become independent.

- Give assistance in "context." Remember, what parents do will affect their other children and their own present and future well-being.
- Point their single-adult child to other resources that may be available to him or her, such as other family members, friends, government agencies, the Church, and the community.
- Let the need for helping their grandchildren override their reluctance to assist a less-than-deserving adult child.
- Not break the law in assisting an adult child (e.g., hiding a grandchild who is the subject of a custody battle) or encourage a son or daughter to do so.
- Not expect their child to "get over it" in a certain period of time. Some things, like certain holidays or events, remain painful indefinitely.
- Err on the side of generosity if they have a question about the "rightness" of what they are doing.

REMARRIAGE, IN-LAWS, AND STEPGRANDCHILDREN

When a son or daughter remarries, it affects all of the family. There is a new personality for the family to get used to, and that new personality has to get used to a family who is accustomed to seeing someone else in his or her shoes. When the new husband or wife brings children into the marriage, that complicates the adjustment for everyone. There are some things that parents of an adult child who has remarried can do to help make this transition, if not smooth, at least doable.

- Put away pictures of the former spouse when an adult child and his or her new spouse are visiting. (This does not mean that parents should not strive to maintain close relationships with the former spouse. They should, but the kind of relationship they will have will be changed.)
- Avoid comparing the new spouse to the former spouse.

- Do not speak disparagingly of the former spouse, especially in front of the new spouse.
- Do not speak disparagingly of the new spouse, especially to the former spouse.
- Put the new spouse and his or her children on birthday and Christmas gift lists.
- Encourage the new spouse to call you "Mom and Dad" and your new stepgrandchildren to call you "Grandma and Grandpa."
- Take family pictures with the new spouse and his or her children, and display them in your home.
- Treat the new spouse as your own child and the step-grandchildren as your natural grandchildren.
- Be patient in the adjustment; it will take time.

While divorce carries with it devastating short- and long-term effects, it is not the end of the world. Every experience, no matter how challenging it may be, can become a tutor, if we will allow it to be so. While such experiences are not usually sought after (unless we have a masochistic bent), they can literally be the road to a fulfilling, even more meaningful life than we had prior to such an experience. That, of course, is a choice. Parents of adult children who are faced with such a choice can play a key role in helping those children survive and even thrive because of what has happened. It is their responsibility to do so.

QUESTIONS & ANSWERS

Q My daughter wants to divorce her husband because she says she doesn't love him anymore. They were married in the temple and are both active in the Church. They have a one-year-old baby. According to my daughter, her husband is a good provider, he's spiritual, and he treats her and the baby great. She just doesn't love him. She claims there is no one else that she is interested in; she just doesn't think it is right that she has to spend the rest of her life and eternity with someone she doesn't love. How should I advise her?

A Tell her she needs to repent. Our counsel here is pretty simple. If your daughter will strive to get her own life in order spiritually, it is likely that her respect and, yes, her love for her husband will begin to grow. She may be "active" in the Church, but it is unlikely that she is praying as she needs to, reading the scriptures on a daily basis, going to the temple often, and losing herself in service. If she were, she would probably be spending much less time thinking about herself and more about the long-term heartache she would bring to this fine husband of hers and her baby if she left. She needs to remember that she has made sacred covenants with him and with the Lord and that she is not justified in pulling up stakes just because she doesn't think she loves him anymore. She will be held accountable for keeping those covenants, and her happiness here and in the eternities literally depends upon it. When she realizes that, she will work to make her present situation better, rather than escaping from it. It sounds like you have a very immature daughter who needs some straightforward counseling from you and from her bishop. Perhaps a marriage counselor would be helpful as well.

Q Our daughter's husband walked out on her and her three children a year ago. He doesn't pay any child support, even though it is court mandated, and she doesn't have any way to make a decent living. She has not been very active in the Church, but has started to come again, maybe so she can get welfare help from the bishop. What is our obligation as parents to help her? We didn't approve of that marriage in the first place, and our daughter hasn't been very close to us for the last five years.

A You need to do everything that you can reasonably do to help her and protect her children (your grandchildren). Consider inviting her and her children to live with you if she will abide by your rules and take advantage of the situation to get an education or training so she can get a job that will provide a livable income. If living with you is not a possibility, consider subsidizing her rent as long as she is following a plan that you have mutually agreed on to prepare her to become a better provider. Work with her bishop to coordinate resources and to help her devise a plan that will ultimately bring her independence. As long as she is willing to do her part, you should be willing to assist. As far as the grandchildren are concerned, you should have as much contact with them as your daughter and they will allow. You can be a great influence on them at this time of their life.

Q Our daughter's husband died, leaving her with the chore of making a living and raising five children. She lives a thousand miles from us and doesn't want to move. We are retired and have very little money to send to her. She seems to be able to put food on the table, but can't keep up with the little jobs around the house that her husband did before he died. She says her house is falling apart, and she doesn't know what to do. A couple of her children are probably old enough to help if they knew what to do, but her husband always did everything himself and never taught them. She is reluctant to ask anyone for help. How can we help her?

A You should consider going to her home for an extended stay to help her get caught up and to do some training of your grandchildren. Call her bishop and explain the situation. Suggest that a home teacher be assigned to her that has the ability and the time and willingness to help with some of these things. Perhaps the home teacher can provide ongoing training for your grandchildren so they can begin to help maintain the house. Then "check up" on them from time to time to see how they are doing. In any case, you need to be involved.

Q We invited our divorced daughter and her four sons to live with us three years ago, and now her teenage boys show no respect to their grandfather and do not abide by his "rules." Our daughter doesn't communicate with us. She has her own room and stays there almost all of the time. She works nights and sleeps days. She is heavily in debt and cannot afford her own place. My husband had open-heart surgery, and this stress is killing him. What do we do?

A Explain to your daughter that it is time for her to be out on her own. Offer to help her put together a budget to better manage her finances and to help her look for a place to live. If you can afford it, you may even want to consider paying the deposit and first month's rent on her new place so that she can move in. Set the time for her to move out (don't give her more than a month or two), and stick to your guns. You are not helping her, her children, and especially not your husband by maintaining the status quo.

Q How does my divorced daughter give her children some good experiences with men without having a man around the house? Her former husband was certainly not the kind of man she wants her children to emulate!

A This is a role that the grandfather can help fill. Your husband should spend as much one-on-one time as possible with these grandchildren. He should not so much try to take the place of their father as to be a super grandfather and a great male image. Your sons and sons-in-law can be a positive influence as well. Good home teachers can also help. Urge your daughter to let them know of her concerns and ask if they would be willing to do things with her children. Importantly, you should counsel your daughter to not be negative about men. It is not uncommon for a divorced woman to become a man-hater, especially a hater of her former spouse. Such an attitude will undermine any attempts by her or others to help her children know and respect men.

Q My son and his wife just recently divorced, and the court awarded custody of their three-year-old son to his mother, even though she uses drugs (she put on a good show for the judge). When my son picks up our grandson every other weekend, he says she is usually stoned, and so is the guy she is living with. Our son wants us to help him find a place out of state where he can take his son and hide from his former wife so he can raise his boy in a good environment. We are just as concerned as our son is about the welfare of our grandson. Should we help our son do this?

A No! What he is talking about doing is called kidnapping, and it is a felony. What you are talking about doing is being an accessory to a kidnapping, and it is also a felony. If you are genuinely concerned about the safety of your grandson, you should counsel your son to go to your county's social service department and issue a complaint. They will do an investigation and, if they consider the environment unsafe, will either force your former daughter-in-law to make certain changes or remove your grandson from the home. Your son may want to consider hiring an attorney who specializes in child law.

Q Our daughter, who is divorced, wants to remarry. She has met a man she says she loves, but his teenage children who live with him treat her like dirt and are mean to her own two children, who are very young. Their father gets after them when they do this and tells our daughter to ignore it, that they will be okay once they are married. We feel uneasy about this. What do you think we should counsel our daughter to do? She asked us.

A You should counsel your daughter not to marry if she sees problems here that she won't be able to live with. She is not just marrying this man that she loves; she is marrying his whole family. The problems you describe are serious enough that she should not count on them being resolved after the marriage. If she can't live with them now, she can be certain that she won't be able to live with them when she has to be in the same house with them without a reprieve. She also needs to consider the effect of constant harassment on her own two children. Unless these problems are settled satisfactorily before the marriage, you can almost be sure the marriage will become a disaster.

Q Our stepgrandchildren (our son's stepchildren) do not accept us. When they are in our home and we tell them to do something, they say they don't have to because we aren't their real grandparents. We want to make them part of our family, but this is hard. What do we do?

A Ask your son and the mother of your stepgrandchildren to fully support your authority in your home. In conjunction with them, establish acceptable consequences if the stepgrandchildren mistreat you or will not obey. Apply the consequences consistently. Express openly your love for your stepgrandchildren and be patient with them. It will take time for the relationship to grow. It may never get to where you want it to be, but it will likely be acceptable. Remember, those children are dealing with rejection themselves, and their reaction to you is natural.

Q Our son has remarried, and his new wife is very uncomfortable around us. She knows how close we are to our former daughter-in-law. We loved his other wife and don't want to lose her friendship, but we are afraid if we don't cut off our relationship with her, our new daughter-in-law will feel threatened and will never be close to us. What should we do?

A You do not have to stop being close friends with your former daughter-in-law. You do need to be careful to not give your new daughter-in-law the impression that you favor your son's former wife over her. Invite your new daughter-in-law over to your home frequently, and try to find out what her interests and likes are. Center your conversations around these. Don't be so self-conscious about it that your conversations become stilted and strained. Put your arm around her and express your love to her. Accept her as a full member of the family. This is a process. Just keep working on it. But don't forfeit your friendship with your son's ex-wife. That is not only unnecessary, but it will likely send an unintended signal to your new daughter-in-law that your relationship is superficial and will terminate if the situation changes. You can imagine the message it will send to your former daughter-in-law, who is already traumatized by her divorce of your son.

CONCLUSION

YOU'RE OKAY!

It is enough to know that we are children of God.

We hope this book has been encouraging as well as helpful. We wanted it to be. We are really talking about the application of the gospel of Jesus Christ here. It is easy to forget that we are still children too. Each stage of our lives is new to us. We haven't done this before (or, at least, not that we remember). Our journey through parenthood is a learning process. We should pursue that journey, having patience in our own stumbling and optimism in its ultimate outcome.

Just as our adult children have an earthly father and mother who care about them and stand ready to help them along their way, so we too have Heavenly Parents, with infinitely more wisdom and understanding than we, who will give us succor and assistance as required. Grace is necessary for us as parents, just as much as it is for our children. That grace is always *sufficient*. Because of this sufficiency, we are helped along our way but, at the same time, able to experience maximum individual growth as well. We are being tutored by divine Parents in whose image we are being fashioned. It is Their example we must strive to follow in dealing with our own adult children.

God bless you in your journey. We know He will. He certainly has blessed us!

ABOUT THE AUTHORS

GARTH A. HANSON is married to Sheila Westover. They have four children and fifteen grandchildren. Garth has served as bishop in three wards, including a young single-adult ward, and he is currently serving as the president of the Romania Bucharest Mission. He received his Ph.D. from the University of Nebraska in Business Education and is an Associate Professor at the BYU Marriott School of Management, Organizational Leadership and Strategy Department. Garth has been a BYU Education Week instructor since 1983, speaking on topics such as "Communicating with Adult Children" and "After a Mission, Then What?" He is the author of several articles for the *Ensign* and coauthor of *Say It Right: A Guide to Effective Oral Business Presentations*.

STEVE D. HANSON is married to Joyce Swenson. They have eight children and twenty-two grandchildren. He has served as a counselor to five bishops and as a stake president's counselor, and he is currently serving as president of the Orange California Stake. He received a bachelor's degree from BYU in Economics and master's degree from Arizona State in Political Behavior. He owns a life insurance and annuity wholesaling business. As a community volunteer, Steve has served as a volunteer in probation for the juvenile justice system of Orange County and is currently serving as a chaplain in the Orange County jail system. Steve is the author of *The Mission* and *Joy, the Other Side of Sorrow*. He is also the author of several articles for the *Ensign* and *This People*.